FATHER'S MILK

Also by André Stein

Hidden Children: Forgotten Survivors of the Holocaust

FATHER'S MILK

NOURISHMENT AND WISDOM FOR THE FIRST-TIME FATHER

ANDRÉ STEIN, Ph.D.
WITH PETER SAMU, M.D.

CAPITAL
BOOKS, INC.
Sterling, Virginia

Capital Books, Inc.
P.O. Box 605
Herndon, Virginia 20172-0605

ISBN 1-892123-77-0 (alk.paper)

Library of Congress Cataloging-in-Publication Data

Stein, André.
    Father's milk : nourishment and wisdom for the first-time father /
André Stein with Peter Samu.
        p.cm
    ISBN 1-18912-377-0 (alk. paper)
    1. Fatherhood. 2. Father and child. I. Samu, Peter. II. Title.

HQ756.S758 2002
306.874'2--dc21

                                                                    2001056185

Printed in the United States of America on acid-free paper that meets the American National Standards Institute Z39-48 Standard.

First Edition

10 9 8 7 6 5 4 3 2 1

CONTENTS

DEDICATIONS

To all the young men, victims of terrorism or war, who have been torn from their children by the enemies of life, and to those who were killed before they even had a chance to taste the joys of being a father. Your bodies lie in darkness; your spirits will forever soar.

To my dad, victim and survivor—forever my dad . . .

To my children, Cybèle, Tristana, Adrian, Eliana, and Sacha—you made it possible for me to be father for you and for me. Without you I wouldn't know what to write in this book, since almost everything I know about fathering I learned from you.

Acknowledgments

Dad, your life was a struggle against the demons of all kinds of darkness. There must have been times when giving up seemed not only tempting but desirable. But not for you. Evil men had robbed you of your sight, but your vision about your children remained clear: "I have to go on; my children need me to go on." Indeed, I needed you to go on, not so much for what you could do for me but just to be there, alive—a witness to my youth and its hills and dales. From you, Dad, I learned the importance of just being there in whatever state. In spite of the numerous ways that the past had poisoned your mind about right and wrong in bringing up children, I learned from you that abandonment was not in your emotional and moral vocabulary. You and I fought a lot. We said hard words to each other. But in some way you must have made it possible for me to speak my mind. In the words of Nobel Peace Prize laureate Elie Wiesel, "the opposite of love is not hate, it's indifference." Not for a moment did I believe that you were indifferent toward me. From you I learned that we have children to be able to give love when we have nothing else to give. Thank you, Dad, wherever else you are, in addition to being in my heart—forever and beyond.

Mom, my dear mom, you were torn from my life when I was so young that at times I believe I'm hallucinating when I think of you. I don't recall the color of your voice, the warmth of your touch, the sweetness of your embrace. I know through the family grapevine that you and Dad were impeccable partners and that he put you ahead of all others. I know that you had a hard life and an incredibly hard death. I remember the words of my father: "I discovered a woman who risked her own life to have me and who loved me more than she loved herself." From you I received a special gift, the joy of giving without expecting something in return. It will have served me faithfully from the first to the last moment of my life. Your name is not mentioned in this book but you are definitely present in every thought.

There were other guides and mentors in helping me choose fatherhood and later the study of fatherhood. Uncle Feri, my high school Hungarian literature and language teacher, you taught me more than anyone certain fundamental truths: to believe in myself, to speak my mind, and to never lose the idea that when all seems dark there is always humor. When the wolves were at my throat, I heard your voice: "Don't let the buzzards get you down. Don't let them crap on your birthday cake." You infused in me the love of written and spoken words, for which I am grateful.

Harvey, my teacher, my mentor, my guide. From you I learned that it is permissible and even necessary to be an imperfect father—indeed, just a person. With the patience of a genuine mentor you inspired in me the concepts that good enough is good enough and to trust my children when they failed to follow the path I had picked for them. That this does not mean rejection but an act of embracing themselves. And if they do that, I have done a good enough job as a father.

Romana, you have come late into my life but not too late. Your reserved but outrageous intelligence and wisdom helped me through some of the many turbulences of my life. You taught me the importance of giving respect and support to one in need, even when you disagreed with his course of actions. You also showed me how to say goodbye, without leaving behind a sense of bereavement or abandonment. From you, I also learned that just as some of the best moms are dads, some of the best dads are moms.

Ed, my agent, what a valiant knight you proved to be. You embraced this project and in spite of running into a wall of visionless editors you stayed the course, steadfastly and courageously. Ed, you are the man!

Noemi, my editor. You and I have never met, and yet I feel I have gained a champion, indeed a friend. Countless times, your elegant assertiveness and compassion made the difference between stress and relief.

And then there are my children, five wonderful human beings, different and yet similar. To each of you I have always given what I had, hardly ever losing sight of the fact that you were a precious being and that my contribution must be in the form of a gift and not a loan. Everything that you'll read in this book, I learned from you. You made it clear what you needed and what you definitely didn't. Plenty of times, I either didn't listen properly or I only thought I listened. Sometimes, I was slow in recognizing your values when they clashed with mine, yet I always knew that you were honest in your pursuit. But at the end of the day we always came back to each other. My father and my mother's father never spoke from the day of my parents' wedding. I can't even imagine such an unbridgeable schism between us, my children, Cybèle, Tristana, Adrian, Eliana, and Sacha. As you said, Adrian, just a couple of days ago, "If I get pissed off at any member of my family, it means nothing to the relationship. We're a family and that's it."

Vicki, my partner, my wife, my friend, my taskmaster, the journey would not have been possible without you by my side. In the truest sense of the word, you are my partner, in joy, struggle, laughter, love, and all undertakings. If I communicate nothing else to my children about marriage and partnership, I hope that they learned from us that marriage is a work in progress, and that when the going gets tough you have to love even more, and that we must never try to win at the expense of the other. The journey is not always a path of rose petals, but I would not be me as a father if you had not been by my side. Thank you for being with me all these years, for the good, the bad, the ugly, and the fun. Children, your mom and I agree that marriage is a package deal. A damned good package and damned good deal.

And finally, I want to acknowledge members of my family who came into my life as a value-added bonus of being married to Vicki. Hilda, my just-departed mother, not mother-in-law. You were the only mother I knew. You were in my life—and deep in it—for twenty-eight years, rich in love, passion, and quiet wisdom. For you, Hilda, my chosen mother, I hope that your spirit knows, wherever its journey takes you, you have enriched my life with your granite commitment to the family, without asking anything in return. I hope that you know, with the spiritual equivalent of knowledge, that your legacy will live on through us.

Lenny and Morty, my brothers through marriage, and Roz and Jessica, your spouses, I want to recognize you also. We have not broken bread as often as I would have liked, and yet I want to acknowledge that your version of dedication to your children and partners has lit the darker corners of my soul. I have found in you kindred spirits. Watching your children growing up, I applaud your child-centered parenting.

—André Stein

My daughter, Dana, has been the most important person in my life since the day she was born, thirty-five years ago. While I have only contributed morsels of knowledge to this book, those I learned from her. And to this day, the morsels keep coming and they're getting bigger. It astounds me in retrospect how ignorantly I came to fatherhood and how I managed to commit every mistake in the book—this book—but not limited to those. Dana is a grownup now, and as we grow closer as we age I still find it almost impossible to silence those voices that want to reclaim her as my child, my child whom I know better than she knows herself, and for whom I know what's good or bad, far better than she knows herself. Fortunately, she knows all this better than I know myself, and she also recognizes that, while I am state-of-the-art, I am also a work-in-progress.

When I was ten, my mother gave me a typewriter the size of a laptop, a feat of miniaturization in its day, the greatest gift (object) I ever received. Soon I was a poet, distributing my works to anyone who stood in one spot long enough, and then waited around anxiously for their critique. She never knew how important a gift my Hermes Baby turned out to be. Of course, all would have been for naught if she hadn't been ready to risk her life for me repeatedly during the war, while I was in hiding on a little farm in Hungary. Only her intelligence and quick wit, along with her fluency in German, saved us from certain extinction.

At eighteen, when I hadn't quite mastered English yet, an English literature teacher at McGill gave me a "C" on an essay about the witches of Salem because she thought my concluding paragraph must have been plagiarized. I was so thrilled at having written something my professor considered too good for me that I now feel I owe her belated gratitude. At the time, however, I only gave her grief.

When I transferred to the University of Toronto the following year, the late Arthur Phelps, a professor beloved and respected by all, called me into his office about an essay I wrote called "Vivisection." There, he handed me back my essay, covered in red ink from all the annotations, but sporting a large circled "A+" on the title page. The reason he called me in, he said, was because he wanted to know a little about me. He was surprised that I spoke with a strong accent. "This essay is good but not A+ material," he said. "I gave you an A+ because I admire your love for the language and your inventiveness." After that, my little typewriter began to have the workouts of its life.

Thomas Verny, M.D., of *The Secret Life of the Unborn* fame, my oldest friend, and a classmate, came to visit me a few weeks after my father's Shivah, and asked to see a story I was writing about my father. After reading it he declared it needed to be published. "Who would publish something like this?" I asked. He thought for a moment and said, "I will." And he did. The result was an anthology of stories about fathers and grandfathers, *Gifts of Our Fathers*, edited by Thomas R. Verny (The Crossing Press, 1994; now out of print). Thanks, Apu, for your life, our relationship, and your support through all the years, one that I often took for granted with youthful arrogance and entitlement.

And then, my good friend André asked me to collaborate in this work. During the endless discussions that ensued, I had the chance to rethink my own role of a father and also to appreciate what my parents must have gone through in raising me and then letting me go to find my wings.

—Peter Samu

PROLOGUE

I'm sixty-five years old and I've been a father for one hundred plus years, adding up the ages of my five children. At times, I feel the weight of that century in my bones, at others, I share the vigor of Sacha who at ten is my youngest. Having the privilege of sharing the lives of these five young people has kept me young and breathless.

During my century of parenting, at one time or another I have probably made every mistake possible. My children have taught me to become a better father with each mistake, and this book is the distillation of what I've learned.

Many a time, the journey was lonely and scary. Mostly, it was hilarious and breathtaking. I have found that there are no green lights and red lights to direct us to the do's and don'ts of fathering. They come in all confusing colors, reminding us that nothing works all the time and that rules are made and broken with sublime subtlety. What I hope to accomplish with this book is to provide a soulful understanding of where the father and the child are coming from and how that influences the point where they meet. Although we cannot hope to completely un-muddy the waters, we can chart a map of where the biggest eddies and whirlpools lie in wait to entrap the unaware. It is my firm belief that truly loving our children means that we have to rise above the lowest common denominator and act in a conscious mode, keeping in mind *their* best interest as well as ours. We must learn to face our limitations, to set realistic expectations for what we can do and what we can't, what is good enough and what is excessive, and ultimately, to have empathy for the child and ourselves.

Thus, this book of practical wisdom for conscious fathers is my gift to all the new fathers who must be as bewildered at the prospect of parenting as I was each time. With all its challenges, crises and pitfalls, I would have not missed being a father for anything in the world. Men, rest assured. There is life after birth.

INTRODUCTION

Fathers, especially first-timers, are in need of guidance and wisdom. Never before has there been such an awareness of glitches in the lives of fathers and their children. Kids complain—in words and in deeds—about missing the active presence of their dads. Women, our partners, are frustrated, disappointed, and even angry. And last, always last, fathers themselves, suspicious and suspected, end up confused, helpless, and all too often . . . absent.

Women have all kinds of support available to them when they become mothers—courses, workshops, TV programs, each other, and most importantly their own mothers. There is a huge amount of literature for expectant mothers. There's very little available for men, and practically nothing that speaks to them with empathy, wisdom, and credibility. The few books on fathering I've been able to find are spiritless manuals. Others are written by women, in a rather condescending and patronizing tone. No matter how well intentioned, female authors only know about the experience of being a father from the fathering they have endured or witnessed. Mixed in with this are pain, bitterness, and solitude.

What new fathers need is guidance from men who have traveled the road, tamed a few beasts, and slain some dragons along the way. Men who have made mistakes and have taken responsibility for them. Men who are courageous, caring, and wise enough to proclaim, at the end of the day: "This is what I've done. This has worked for me and will probably work for you. But stay away from that."

The younger fathers also need to learn from their seniors to clarify their values and perspectives and consequently relax a little. It is time to dispel the notion that they have to work themselves to death to provide the best of everything for their families. Guilt-driven silent tracks are playing in their brains: "Be the best father in the whole wide world! Your child must have everything money can buy! Your child must lead a perfect life! You didn't have it so good . . . your kid will make up for it." The simple truth is that a father must not do anything that will leave him exhausted, frustrated, and bitter at the end of the day; otherwise, sooner or later, he will fall casualty to the disease of the gender: absenteeism.

Being a father is complex, challenging, and at times, bewildering. Attitudes and behaviors that thirty years ago would have earned a man a father-of-the-year award are now labeled overbearing and sexist. Men have to adapt to hands-on, active, and competent fathering, but nothing in their past has prepared them for the task, nor do they have anywhere to turn for help.

Men are saddled first of all with the myth that they lack the biological wherewithal to be front-line nurturers and caregivers, something that women are granted as standard equipment. This of course is a falsehood that has achieved unwarranted acceptance in our culture.

Men need to hear male voices refuting such myths with authority and wisdom. It is essential that men embark on the magical journey of fatherhood without being weighted down by self-doubts about suitability, ability, and competence. All a father needs, to be actively involved in nurturing, is volition. There is no equipment missing. Fathers can become nurturing fathers, and some of the best mothers I've known were men.

But not all. Let me tell you a story about my father. He was a good man, a victim of a time that failed to prepare most men for the role and joy of nurturing. The story goes back some thirty-five years.

My first-born child, Cybèle, is ten days old and something is terribly wrong. My wife and I pack her into the car and rush her down to the Children's Hospital in the middle of the night. She is very ill, but no one seems to know what's wrong. We watch her through the glass wall, in intensive care—tubes and electrodes everywhere. This goes on for two days. Finally, I must tear myself away to pick up my father at the airport.

He is flying in to lend me moral support, I'm thinking. I feel gratitude welling up inside me. We've not had a smooth father-son relationship so far, but I'm in desperate need.

I am pacing up and down in the arrival lounge at Oakland International Airport, disoriented with panic and fear. I spot him at last, an inch shorter than I remember him. It's been a couple of years.

I start walking toward him. He hasn't seen me yet. What I'm thirsting for is a hug, an infusion of strength to rebuild my resilience and optimism. My father, a man who has suffered so much in his life, surely must have a reservoir of compassion and wisdom for just such emergencies. I rush eagerly to embrace him.

"How is she?" he asks matter-of-factly after a furtive and evasive hug. He stiffly pushes me away. I hardly catch a sniff of his aftershave, a scent that has been a fixture of my memory of him to this day.

"What kind of doctors do you have here anyway?" he asks. "Do they know anything?"

I don't want an exchange of words, a discussion about my daughter's medical condition. What I need more than anything is a father's reassuring embrace, words of sympathy, and understanding. Hope against hope, I want desperately to hear, "I'm here, my son, and we'll face this together."

I try again.

"Dad, thanks for coming." I put my arm around his shoulder.

"Get a hold of yourself, people are watching." He holds me at arm's length.

My daughter thankfully survived to grow into a healthy and beautiful young woman, although we never learned the name of the bug that almost killed her. I've just finished talking to her on the phone, which I do almost every day. I was reminiscing, having just written this intro, probably not the first time, about my late father's visit to Berkeley. "Brrr," she shivered on the phone. "What made him so cold and unfeeling? I can't ever imagine you being like that."

Soothing words for this father to hear.

Men (and women), you've probably heard it said, often become replicas of their parents. For men at least, this is generally not a good thing. Times are changing rapidly for men and for women. Yesterday's response is hopelessly out of date. The status of the father of the family as ruler has vanished, probably for a variety of reasons but mostly because now two people bring home the bacon.

Men, much of this book is designed to help you avoid falling into the trap of passing on inappropriate messages you've heard in your childhood. You have adopted these without understanding. Many of these time-bombs are handed down unconsciously through generations. My aim is to make you aware of the devilishly crafty influences that, to your own amazement, make you behave in hurtful ways toward your child and toward yourself. If you are about to become a father or have recently become one, standing there confused, scared, and insecure about your ability to carry this out effectively, then this book is for you. If on the other hand you think you can trust your instincts, if you think it doesn't take conscious effort, if you think you can do it by going with the flow, then you won't feel the need for any kind of advice and you'll seek only your own counsel. Reading this book, however, may make you reconsider.

This book contains hundreds of pieces of wisdom to help you out in the kind of challenging and problematic situations every father faces at one time or another. Rather than leaving you to discover them alone, I offer to accompany you as your guide, a guide with a hundred years of personal child-raising experience. I was also in the fortunate position to learn from many of my clients, who have come to me for myriad reasons, and from their children. These lessons have become part of my knowledge, made available to you here as your guide.

Rather than hiding a problem in a far corner of your mind hoping it will go away, which never happens for very long, you can develop the assurance to confront each new problem as it arises and resolve it, secure in the knowledge that you and your family will get through the process essentially undamaged.

Perhaps the most important piece of wisdom that you will find in this book is that on this journey of being a father, there is a need for constant refinement and fine tuning. Just as you can never take your relationship with your partner for granted, that is, if you want it to be exciting, lively, and romantic, you cannot take for granted your latest, new-and-improved version of fathering. Just when you think you've got it down pat, your child grows another day. When you wake up, someone has changed the scenery and a new set of props has sprouted on the stage.

FATHER QUOTIENT QUESTIONNAIRE

Answer yes or no to the following questions:

1. Do you have (or want to have) a child because you feel you should?

2. Is it important for you to live with your companion in an equal partnership?

3. Are you prepared to temporarily put yourself last?

4. Do you have the courage to experience all emotions?

5. Is the gender of your baby very important to you?

6. Can you see yourself as a "pregnant father"?

7. Is participating in every phase of your child's life a given for you?

8. Your partner will be an active player in your baby's delivery. Will you?

9. Are you grossed out at the very thought of changing your baby's diapers?

10. Do you resent your child interfering with your sex life?

11. Is it very important to you that your child be like you?

12. Do you think it's inevitable that you will be parenting like your father did?

13. Do you believe in inflicting pain on your child for his or her own good?

14. Excepting the risk of physical danger, do you think it necessary to think before acting?

15. Are you prepared to give up some sleep to make it possible for your child to fall or stay asleep?

16. Do you believe in the value of having regular times set aside for just your partner and you?

17. Can you be loving when your child acts in a way that's unlovable?

18. Are you prepared to give up an important sporting event to attend your child's sporting event?

19. Are you always right and your child is always wrong?

20. Do you believe in the value of finding a mentor to help you with fathering?

ANSWERS
(1) no, (2) yes, (3) yes, (4) yes, (5) no, (6) yes, (7) yes, (8) yes, (9) no, (10) no, (11) no, (12) no, (13) no, (14) yes, (15) yes, (16) yes, (17) yes, (18) yes, (19) no, (20) yes

FATHER QUOTIENT

If you answered 16 or more correctly, you could be a candidate for the Father of the Year Award.

If you answered 11 to 15 correctly, you are definitely on the right track. With some guidance, you'll be a good father.

If you answered 6 to 10 correctly, you need some empathic and wise parenting education from a fathering mentor who believes that fathers are as important in a child's life as are mothers. You'll also benefit from talking to and observing fathers who love to be involved with their child even when it hurts to do so.

If you answered less than 6 correctly, you're definitely the weakest link in your child's life. Unless you take a deep and sustained look at your version of parenting, one day your child will make a psychotherapist very happy.

Regardless of your Father Quotient, you will benefit from reading *Father's Milk* for information when the going gets rough or for re-enforcement and fine tuning when all is going well in your home.

PART I

FATHER
AND HIS PARTNER

CHAPTER 1

LEARN TO SWIM IN ESTROGEN

The moment you find out that your mate is in a family way, the level of female hormone in your household rises like the waters of a sleepy river in the spring. This happens quite innocently and it's all perfectly understandable, but unless you're prepared, you could find yourself in deep water. What we'll learn in this chapter is how to develop a healthy resistance to the ill effects of estrogen on the male psyche, so that we can stay afloat and even frolic in it safely.

As soon as the lab test turns positive, a number of automatic systems are triggered into action:

1. All the female friends you or your partner have ever known are telepathically informed that a baby's on the way and begin phoning your house.

2. Your mother-in-law and seven sisters-in-law make sure to call daily to check on your partner's progress. Should you accidentally answer the phone, you will likely be encouraged to assume more of the household duties.

3. Conversation in any social situation quickly turns to natural birthing, Lamaze, midwives, and obstetricians. You will learn all the details, with or without your expressing interest, about your neighbor's labor with each of her children.

And all this before D-day ("D" for delivery).

In the course of the next seven or eight months, your partner unwittingly becomes the star of a developing drama, as you fade into the background. It's all so natural and so benign that most likely you won't even notice at first. After all, you're a gallant and magnanimous soul, the last person in the world to begrudge your partner the enjoyment of the miraculous transformation occurring in her tummy. And it's your baby too! So you allow yourself to be swept along by warm currents, buoyed by the excitement of the impending addition to the family.

But the imbalance may eventually make you feel excluded and neglected, and should it catch you unprepared, you will grow to resent the lack of attention from your partner, as well as the invasion of your space by her friends and relatives. And the flood lasts a long time: the eight or so months of confinement (the first month you were blissfully ignorant of what's coming), and several months after delivery.

This may be counterintuitive, but for very sound reasons it would be unwise to tinker with this imbalance. Let's stop for a moment thinking about ourselves and consider what our partner is going through. Just imagine if it were one of us who had to *carry* the baby! The thought of it alone is likely to send us cowering into a dark corner. Have you ever stopped to wonder how she manages to do it with such ease and dignity? Wouldn't we be bitching and complaining, louder and more franticly each day as D-day approached? And imagine the effect on our vanity of seeing those stretch lines for the first time and knowing that sometimes they're there for life, standing on a scale horrified at the extra weight, making all those trips to the bathroom, and trying to avoid the fiendish mirrors that pop up unexpectedly, showing our bloated bodies and puffy faces.

That phenomenon, where a woman's joy of expecting a baby can completely block the fear of carrying and delivering it, is in my opinion the real miracle of childbirth. Somehow, in spite of bodily discomforts, our partner grows more serene and blissful as the date approaches. How does she do it?

For one, she doesn't do it in a vacuum; she needs the company of other women, that extra dose of "woman" to prepare her for the physical and emotional climax of giving birth. Women have a special gift, an ability to pass on each other's strength by simply sharing experiences. By telling each other their joys and sorrows, their excitement and anxiety, the sisterhood gains force and infuses itself into your partner.

Have you really listened to a conversation between two women? Women talk differently from us. They don't come to the point in a straight line. They cover vast territories, like birds on a thermal, as if the journey were more important than getting there. You don't see one woman interrupting the other with "Come on. Get to the point."

The secret as usual is in the small print. If you listen carefully, you will hear little revelations, almost unintended clues about themselves, who they are, how they cope, their emotions, what's important, and what isn't. The more they reveal about themselves, the stronger becomes the bond between them. The larger the surface, the better the glue sticks. To deny your partner that opportunity means weakening her for the task ahead.

During pregnancy, a woman's body secretes hormones that allow the pelvic ligaments to stretch without tearing. I wouldn't be surprised if an as yet undiscovered substance worked a similar magic on her brain, refocusing the mind and steeling her resolve for what looks to me from where I sit an almost superhuman task, not only carrying but d-e-l-i-v-e-r-i-n-g the baby.

If for no other reason than preserving your own sanity, you want your partner to be as strong as possible. Especially if you are in the habit of relying on her to keep you on an even keel. It may be a good idea, by the way, to begin looking elsewhere, to a good male friend, a counselor, an older brother, or a clued-in doctor.

Too bad we men can't join in with the women for support. Women's style of conversation does not work for us. It makes us edgy, and we tend to leave the room to watch TV or read the paper. We sometimes seem to behave, particularly when stressed, as if we were above feelings. Like Carly Simon in her song decrying her mate's attitude, "We don't need love at all."

Needless to say, all is not as it appears. Something makes us shove our feelings down as quickly as they arise, into a locked piggy bank to which we have lost the key. Actually, the key was not lost. It got thrown away by adults who taught us how boys were expected to behave in emotional situations.

When surrounded by women, exercising their camaraderie, we are faced with a choice: we can listen to the voices around us or to the silence inside us. My recommendation is to listen with an open mind. But you can't forget who you are, because what this calls for is a delicate balance.

You can be seduced by estrogen. Too much of it can compromise your male energy. You, the hunter of the hunter-gatherer duo, have emerged as the sentinel of danger. You size up a situation and quickly move to action. That's your job. You can't afford to become what Robert Bly calls the "soft, new-age male."

When my wife was pregnant with our second child, despite the overall joy of the occasion I was preoccupied with the diminished quality of life we might be facing with not one but, imagine, two children. My wife was my best and my only bosom buddy, so I told her how I felt. Bad move. To this day I clearly remember her reply: "You have no right to be scared. If you're scared, it means there's a reason to be scared and that freaks me out."

It may be a manly thing to look out beyond the horizon for whatever is or may be a threat in the future. Our fears run interference with our enjoyment of the moment—the price we pay for having clear, testosterone-driven logical minds. However, it is not necessary to paint the devil on the wall and share every fear. My wife needed me fearless when it came to the children. She already had more on her plate than she could handle. Unavoidably, there are issues you just cannot discuss with your partner, especially when her mind is set on nesting.

If your partner is your best friend, that's great. But if she is your only intimate friend, you are in trouble. Regardless of how close you are to your partner, it is not enough, especially now. Her line is busy.

Find one or two fellow travelers who also have pregnant wives. You've probably never had a heart-to-heart talk with anyone about where your life was going now that you were to become a father. Don't be surprised if your friend is also starving for an audience, even if he doesn't know it yet.

In my clinical practice, when I recommend to prospective fathers that they spend time in the company of other like-minded, soulful men, the standard responses are: "I ain't got the time. I don't talk to men about that sort of thing. I don't know any men." Of course, what they are really saying is: "You're full of shit. I have more important things to do."

The ones that follow my advice are invariably grateful for it. For the fact of the matter is that heart-to-heart talks with other men, while staying off the beaten track of weather, sports, politics, stock market, martinis, and other women, help maintain your maleness in your female-dominated world. This in turn allows your partner to go unencumbered where she needs to go at this time. Then, whenever the two of you get together, you meet on equal terms, male and female, without gender shifting, in the natural way that you have always related.

Not any man will do, of course. Avoid like the plague men (and women) who come out of the woodwork to pollute your horizon with horror. You need to hear empowering rather than nightmarish stories. Make sure the men in your life are of good will and that at least one of them has gone through the experience of parenting and lived to tell a terrific story.

CHAPTER 2

CHILDREN ARE NOT ASSETS

Years ago, I saw a French cartoon in which one man was standing on a hilltop, gesturing all around, showing off to another: "My castle . . . my car . . . my horses . . . my kids," pointing to all his possessions. The other turned his back and patted his backside: "My ass!" I'm always reminded of this cartoon when I hear or see someone referring to his child in proprietary tones, with some even claiming: "My children are my most important assets."

Real estate, gold, stocks, and bonds are assets. They have commercial value and can be converted into cash. We no longer do that with our children. Their value lies in their intrinsic worth, which is incalculable and is certainly not measured in how much they do or do not enrich our lives.

The idea of "having" children is an unfortunate choice of words that legitimizes ownership, even if only in a manner of speaking. It is so ingrained in our culture that no one bats an eyelash. But we cannot "have" what does not belong to us. But maybe I'm making too much of it because the idea of slavery in any form infuriates me.

We contribute the semen and our partner an ovum. Both are randomly picked from a basket we inherited, outside of our consciousness, outside of our control. To claim either creative input or possession is an arrogant affront to Mother Nature.

And yet, we all tend to think of our kids as belonging to us—which does not serve them well, since the ways we tend to express ownership are bad for our children's self-image. When we slap them, however lightly, or when we behave towards them in ways that we ourselves would find demeaning, or when we turn them into performing monkeys, as in beauty pageants, we are expressing ownership. Whenever we say, "Do this because I'm your father," we're implying ownership. We think of our children as assets when we make them do things solely for our own sake, to improve the quality of our lives. Or when we treat them as invisibles when it suits us, as at the dinner table, for example, when we chit-chat about work, taxes, or sex as if they weren't even part of the household.

I hate to harp on my father (although as you see I do it quite a lot), who isn't here to defend himself. But if he were, I would be intimidated, and this book would never have been written. My father was highly disapproving of my parenting style, among other things. When I visited him in Budapest with my three-year-old daughter, whom he hadn't seen since she was a baby, my father wanted her to kiss him. "Kiss Grandpa!" he demanded, as my daughter shrank into as tiny a speck as she could manage.

"But, Dad," I said, "she doesn't know you."

He answered curtly, "She should do as she's told." My poor father never got his kiss. And my poor daughter never got to kiss her grandfather.

I often think of the patriarch Abraham, whom God challenged to stab to death his beloved son Isaac, and then burn his body as an offering to the Heavenly Father. Why? To prove that his love for God was boundless. Here resides a heinous instance of paternal ownership, which men through centuries have yet to live down.

Instead of owning my children, I think of them as being loaned to me for safekeeping. This means that I cannot exploit them for my own purposes. It also means that when the time comes for them to leave the family nest they must be in at least as good a shape as when they arrived.

What does this mean to a new father? It means we have to allow the child to determine the direction his budding life will take. Our job is to provide a safe and nourishing home. Because of genetics, and through the process of just living together, similarities in interests and abilities are likely to emerge between you and your child. As gratifying as this may feel at the time, it does not mean that the child should be encouraged to develop into a miniature replica of you. He must be allowed to grow without the impositions of your dreams and expectations. Being nonjudgmental towards your child's leanings is another of those difficult tasks for the new father to master.

I work very hard at not being the kind of parent who thinks he is the ultimate authority on what's good for the children. Kids already know inside what feels right and what doesn't. During my one-hundred-plus cumulative years of being a father, there couldn't have been more than a dozen occasions when I imposed my will through sheer authority, or just because I was bigger and stronger.

I do break my own rule when the child is too young to reason with or when facing physical danger. Paternal (or maternal for that matter) authority is usually a shortcut to spending sufficient time with your child to make your point of view understood.

Yet, I'm not the kind of father who allows his children unlimited freedom. Everyone has a zone of comfort of what is acceptable and what is not. You cannot step too far out of this zone without becoming an irritable wreck. The children instinctively recognize your boundaries and spend considerable time testing the limits. Which is how it should be. Children develop survival muscles from this exercise. Sometimes you yield a little, and sometime you put your foot down.

Nor am I the kind of father who tries to become a buddy to his child, although I've caught myself straying in that direction now and then. The problem with being a buddy is twofold. First, you deprive your child of the parent, whom he needs a lot more than he needs a friend. And second, it's impossible to maintain the posture for very long because after all you're not twelve, or sixteen, or twenty-one. These quick transitions from one role to the other are disorienting to you both and in the end will likely damage your relationship.

The line between a buddy and a parent is sometimes a very fine line. That's why it takes time to recognize it and then to learn not to cross it. But the alternative, which I definitely do not recommend, is sitting at the parental throne and treating your children as subjects. There's no green light or red light to guide you, since life spews out challenges in every color of the spectrum. In my view, the ideal relationship between a father and a child is one of mutual respect, yet recognizing the father as a couple of steps higher in the pecking order. Absolute equality leads to absolute mayhem, while an authoritarian division leads to coldness and distance.

By natural inclination, I sometimes find myself drifting too close to equality, only to be rudely reminded that it's time to ratchet up myself a couple of notches. If I then drift the other way, which for me does not come easily, the distance is too cold to bear. Since almost everything of real value I continue learning from my kids, I miss those qualities when I become too dictatorial—such as unconditional love, vulnerability, innocent mischief, trust, faith in immortality, the primacy of the moment, lust for strong experiences, unbridled fantasy, and most importantly, belief in a world where everything is made of chocolate.

CHAPTER 3

SOME OF THE BEST MOMS ARE MEN

There is a nasty myth out there that men are not nurturers. And yet, millions of women enter into long-term relationships with men. Could all these women have been led astray?

I'd venture to say that a large majority of women do get a good measure of the warmth, understanding, sensitivity, generosity, strength, affection, and security they crave from their partners. Which can only mean that somewhere inside us we possess those qualities, even if we have to dig deep to find them. And if we are able to give those qualities to another man's daughter, we can certainly do the same for our own children.

Nature, in designing men and women as specialists, has not seen fit to grant man the role of primary nurturer. It befell us to be the hunters and protectors. Hence our arms bulge with bigger muscles and our brains can calculate the trajectory of a missile to bring down the woolly mammoth. Men may start as the same glob of tissue inside the womb, but when bombarded with testosterone pellets they become little Sherman tanks. But don't count out the heart of a warm, wet puppy beating inside. It's just that if we show too much sensitivity it gets pummeled out of us at school, or by our siblings, or by our dads and, yes, even our moms. And if we still haven't learned our lesson, there's always the military.

The downside of specialization is that we have allowed ourselves to be locked out of the nursery. And we are still hanging out there to dry. The Bible hasn't helped, either. As I have alluded to in another chapter, Abraham, the quintessential model of wisdom and maturity, had his blade unsheathed and poised to execute his son—an action some mothers would interpret as lacking in sensitivity. There are other examples in the Good Book of male characters whose nurturing attributes could be called into question. In the context of today's mores, a mother might have difficulty with the concept of human sacrifice, especially of her child. What I know for sure is that the Bible has set the tone for a steep, uphill battle for fathers as nurturers.

We are prejudged as heartless and calculating. It's as if each father had to reinvent fatherhood in order to prove himself worthy. So, what can we do to put "daddy" back into father? I can tell you a little something that's worked for me and many of the men I've counseled in my practice.

It involves using the part of our makeup with which nature has endowed us generously: the power of reasoning and carrying out a preconceived plan. Men are best at effecting change once they have consciously identified the problem. No amount of outside nagging and cajoling is as effective as insight.

In this case the problem might be stated like this. Our rough exterior (speech, manner, and appearance) makes us appear unlikely nurturers. Something must be done to change this perception. The next step is to develop a plan of action. If this sounds calculating, it's the way our testosterone-driven brain is designed.

If we think of the time we spend with our kid as a personal sacrifice, it only means we haven't been spending enough time alone with him or her. There is a temptation (I've been there) to use the time we're spending with our children as an occasion to catch up on the tasks we would be doing otherwise, hoping they will amuse themselves or, even better, fall asleep. This is not only cheating but counterproductive. The idea is to use every opportunity to get closer to our children. For only then does the magic begin; only then can we genuinely begin to enjoy.

Women tend to know a lot more about babies because it's their specialty. They are groomed for nurturing from the word go—by moms, nurses, teachers, and the rest of humanity. They're given dolls to play with. They read stories about families and relationships. There are hundreds of mothering books for each fathering title. But it's not too late for us to learn. All we need to do is declare it a priority.

One of the most significant times I've ever spent with my son was when he was seven and came down with a nasty case of strep throat . . . high fever, huge tonsils, the works. We were supposed to be attending a wedding in Vermont and had been talking about the trip for weeks. I swallowed hard and declared that I would stay home with my son. I have to tell you that this was not without a sense of sacrifice.

What I gained during those five days was an unexpected glimpse of what motherhood must be like. My son sat in my lap for as long as *he* wanted. I *alone* had to attend to all his needs.

While the experience made me feel competent and life-sustaining, it was initially an exhausting and lonely task. I was even feeling resentful, which came as a bit of a shock, that my wife was out there having a carefree time. It's a peculiar mix of being stranded by one's own volition and at the same time yearning to be free, if even for a moment. It's the way I imagine moms feel much of the time.

But toward the end of the weekend as my son started to improve, we both began to have a close and wonderful time. We laughed, played games, read stories, and never even turned on the TV. The initial sacrifice paid off in droves.

When my family came back, I could honestly tell my wife that the weekend had been just great and I wouldn't have swapped it for five Vermonts.

CHAPTER 4

SHE LOVES ME, SHE LOVES ME NOT

The baby has been home for several weeks now, sleeping quietly in her crib next door, while your partner has collapsed beside you on the bed. It's eleven o'clock. Earlier, you'd arrived bearing flowers; you were your most charming all evening; you washed *and* dried the dishes, asked all about her day, all the while testosterone was overflowing into your bloodstream. Finally, you can stand it no longer. You reach out as gently and tentatively as you can. But it's a no go! She shrinks back from your touch; obviously she doesn't love you anymore. "Now that she's got her kid," you figure, "she's got no more use for me."

Well, yes and no. Your baby and your partner have been together for nine months while you stood on the outside looking in— albeit solicitously. Her immediate focus is naturally the baby. Nine months is a long time. For quite some time after delivery, mother and child are still one body, as if accidentally separated. You cannot and really shouldn't try to insert yourself between them. For the moment, she might as well still be pregnant. The difference is that she is eager to introduce the baby to you. She will rejoice at your acceptance and delight in your joy. The love she directs at you, for the time being, is through the baby. Once you demonstrate your full acceptance of the child's being in the home and you show yourself as a careful and capable custodian, she will be able to relax and direct some of her energy toward you.

If before you were the apple of her eye, you may have just become a very fine tomato. Both have a unique and separate place at your table, just as you and the baby occupy different compartments in her heart. If earlier she would have jumped in front of an eighteen-wheeler for you, the heart may still be willing but since that would make your child an orphan, a bit of caution is now in order. Think of it not as a demotion but a lateral shift. What the baby's arrival forces upon you both is to think long term. The quick fix you had in mind does not qualify.

One of the discoveries you are bound to make because of this lateral shift is that you are a lot less tough and secure than you thought possible. You have just gone through the pregnancy and the delivery. While not as traumatic as it was for her, there were moments now and then of your own private hell. You did everything right. You were supportive, loving, and tolerant. So where's your reward? You seem to be losing out. You feel as if her love for you died with the birth of your baby.

When I had just become a father for the first time, I watched my wife looking at our baby with eyes melting with passion, tenderness, and fulfillment—the kind of look she used to reserve for me after a night of extraordinary passion. This literally wet-behind-the-ears ragamuffin seems to set ablaze her entire universe without the least personal effort, with just a smile, a gurgle, a squeak, or doing nothing at all. My reason told me that I was in a much better position than when there were only two of us, but jealousy and feelings of abandonment at first prevented me from full enjoyment. If none of this sounds familiar, you're either not there yet or you have already mercifully forgotten.

If you're not there yet, I have good news and bad news. First, the bad news: no, you cannot compete with your baby. Not now, not ever. The good news is you don't have to. Resist the temptation of feeling sorry for yourself, ending up resenting the mother-child union. If you try competing with your child, not only will you lose, but you will also make the three of you extraordinarily miserable in the process. Certainly, your partner's life will be hell trying to satisfy your needs as if you were another baby.

During this period after my first child was born, I was fortunate to have a pediatrician in San Francisco who became my mentor for many years. I don't know if it was something he said or whether I came to it on my own, but after a long conversation with him it finally dawned on me that regardless of how much I nagged and complained I could never reclaim the exclusive place in my wife's heart I once possessed. It just wasn't in the cards. I must stop feeling sorry for myself and try to assume the new stance of an active and supportive husband *and* father.

This realization did not instantly convert to action. It took a few months before my mind wrapped itself around the new reality. Not long after I stopped demanding it (silently, with dog eyes only), my wife's interest in sex miraculously resurfaced. Then, as I regained some security in our relationship, I started seeing the wife-baby union as another member of the family. I became a supporting member of a three-legged stool and thus began my transformation into a family man. What I gained was a new relationship—a kind of threesome that more than made up for the lateral shift I'd sustained.

Soon, you too will be broadcasting your new elation about being a father. For instance, you will find yourself creating a new universe that only you and your child inhabit. Just the two of you. The raw, unselfish love you will feel for your child is unlike any you have known before. It is the glue that holds the world together.

The day will come when, instead of raining on everyone's parade, you will lighten up. All you have to do is look at your baby's smiling face, and in her eyes you'll see sunshine, your guiding light.

CHAPTER 5

COUNT ME IN

"Emily, if you don't stop working all those hours, I'll tell Dawn that you don't care to spend time with her. I swear it." Ken was relaying his words about a recent discussion with his wife, Emily, a super-ambitious vice president of sales at a BMW dealership. "I know it's not noble or even wise, and I doubt if I would ever do it," he said, "but isn't it true? I might as well be a single father! Dawn, at four, has been practically motherless for six days out of the week. Emily even missed her birthday party because the Big Cheese wanted her for some shit campaign. I'm sick of it. Dawn may as well learn the truth about her mother sooner rather than later."

"You sound bitter, betrayed and vengeful," I offered, "and perhaps with good reason. But you conspire against her in a way that can only be hurtful to Dawn. To break Dawn's heart telling her that her mother doesn't love her sounds like emotional cruelty. What does that make you? A kind, loving, empathic, wise dad? Not likely. Her mom abandons her physically while you attack her emotionally by telling her in so many words that she is worthless and unlovable. At first blush this seems like a kind of blackmail in which everybody loses, especially Dawn."

"I don't know what else to do. I have no problem being the homemaker, but I won't settle for being a chump either. By the time I have a free minute, after her bedtime, I'm too exhausted to write. I also have a schedule to meet. Don't I count? I'm also tired of lying to Dawnie at the end of the day that Mommy will be home any minute when I know she won't be home until ten. I'm at the end of my wits. I can't do it any more, and I won't. This is war!"

"So I see . . . and your daughter is the hostage and ammunition."

This type of situation has been arising more frequently in my practice, since family and parental roles are in a state of flux. More often it is the woman who feels neglected. These three obviously need help.

The best kind of help would leave the child out of the conflict. The predicament is 100 percent adult-made. The child bears no responsibility, nor can she do anything about it.

The first thing to do, Kevin and I concluded, was to level with his wife and express his frustration, hurt, and anger in a way that Emily could hear without feeling attacked. More than likely she already feels guilty and has built up her defenses to the hilt. The shakier her defenses, the more vigorously she will stick to them, for she cannot afford to cast further doubts on her lifestyle and its effect on the family. The slightest crack would collapse her house of cards, and then where would she be? Facing radical change— something that would clash head-on with her ambition and un-quenchable thirst for approval and success in the outside world.

We had rehearsed several scenarios for the "discussion," with me taking Emily's role, until it became obvious that Kevin would be unable to carry out his mission without becoming hostile and agitated, thus precipitating a huge fight. Instead, he would invite Emily for a joint counseling session.

Fortunately, she agreed. I began by asking each of them to de-scribe what they would want for themselves and their family in an ideal setting, without financial constraints. In other words, what was most important for each of them, a process known as "value clarification."

When they had finished, they looked at each other quietly for a minute and then burst out laughing. And I had to join in because it was genuinely funny the way they came up with an almost iden-tical list.

I asked them next to consider what would they be willing to give up, change, and sacrifice to be consistent with their values. We spent some time exploring Emily's overriding ambition. For an in-depth understanding of how she got into her current predicament, I referred her to a colleague for individual counseling, to which she was receptive.

When that was done, I asked them to set a date when they'd implement the plan.

This was met by an outburst from Emily. How dare I suggest that she give up her $186,000 job after a few minutes of "chatting"? Who did I think I was, anyway!

This was good because I deflected her anger. Kevin stood up and supportively placed his hand on her shoulder, and she folded her palm over his hand. When she'd calmed down and Kevin had returned to his seat, she looked at him softly and was able to see, perhaps for the first time, the despair and helplessness in her husband's eyes. And that in turn gave him permission to begin sobbing quietly, something he had never done in front of her.

He began to speak about Dawn, a very sad little girl, who didn't dare to show how sad and even angry she was at her mommy for spending so little time with her. How she could not afford to voice her loneliness for fear of jeopardizing the little time she had with her mother. "Besides," he said, turning to Emily, "she loves you so much that she would never want you to feel bad."

Emily grew pensive. Then she too shed some quiet tears. "I'm sorry. This should never have happened. We have to do something. . . ."

Very recently I had an opportunity to deal with a similar crisis in the making. It may seem that I am pointing the finger at women in this chapter, but that is not my intention. I am just going where my clientele takes me. Besides, for every culprit there is a consenting party, who has a significant share in perpetuating and sometimes unwittingly encouraging the offence.

My client James, an insurance broker, frustrated by his wife's version of family culture, excluding him from almost everything to do with their child, began coming home less and less. He was particularly resentful of her habit of spending an hour or two putting their six-year-old to bed. Whenever he tried walking in, they stopped talking and he was forced to withdraw. He felt so undervalued and invisible in his own home that he started to work seven days a week.

Barb, his wife, felt hurt and rejected by this and when little Bobby asked one day, "Where's Daddy?" she answered, "I don't know, I think he doesn't live here anymore." Bobby was devastated. With the usual self-centeredness of children, he thought Daddy had left because he had been a bad little boy and daddies only love good little boys.

When James came home that night, he walked in on Bobby and Barb's nightly ritual. Expecting cold indifference, he was stunned when Bobby sat bolt upright and shouted, "Daddy, Daddy, you came back! I didn't want to be bad."

James was so deeply touched that he found the courage to ask his wife to leave the room. "I want to talk to my son," he said firmly.

He sat on the bed and gently installed Bobby on his lap. "Sweetheart, my baby, I'm not going anywhere. If Mommy told you I was leaving, she must have been joking. Not a very good joke, mind you, don't you agree? You're a wonderful boy. And even if you did something very bad, I'd still love you and I would never leave you." By the time he finished, Bobby had heard enough to make him feel secure, as he fell instantly asleep.

His wife, when confronted later, said, "You're home so little that I'm not sure you still live here."

"So you take it out on Bobby."

But what he really thought was, "I've been spending less and less time at home because I feel devalued and excluded. You've shown me in countless ways that since Bobby arrived, I've become nothing more than a bottomless wallet. You don't have the time of day for me, except when you want me to fix the lawn mower. And if you don't have a chore for me you go to sleep 'exhausted.' I've asked you countless times, 'let's go out on a date.' But you want Bobby along. When I suggested spending a week in Club Med, you would only go if kids were welcome. Don't you think I love Bobby as much as you do? The last few times—I stopped counting—when I wanted to make love, you brushed me off because we would wake Bobby. Shall I go on? You set our son between us. So I go to the office where I am useful and where I'm liked."

This couple didn't solve their problem. For one thing, Barb refused couple counseling. She didn't think there was anything wrong with putting her kid first.

James eventually retained the services of a family lawyer-mediator and initiated separation proceedings, requesting joint custody. Having failed mediation, they ended up in court. Due to the custody imposed by the court, James was unable to keep the promise he had made to his son that he would never leave him. He moved out and saw his son three times a week and alternate weekends.

When giants wage war, the little people suffer. And it doesn't stop there. The hurt carries on and shapes future relationships and therefore future generations. Think twice about going to war. And above all seek counseling before you find yourself on the brink.

CHAPTER 6

BRING HOME MORE THAN
THE BACON

The "absent father" is very much in the news today. Since fathers work long hours away from home they are likely to become visitors in their own homes, hardly catching up with their child while he is awake, morning or night. A lot of fathers are absent from their kids' lives even when they are present. This is seldom intentional. (I'm one of those people who think that human beings are fundamentally good, until proven otherwise.)

The purpose at hand is to offer help for inexperienced, confused, or befuddled first-time dads, to stop them from leaving home or being absent without leaving, and to bring them in from the cold if they find themselves outside.

Since the beginning of time, some would argue because of Nature's survival-oriented delegation of duties, Dad has assumed the role of the hunter and was therefore in charge of bringing home the bacon. Things have changed in the last generation or two. Now, in most families, two wage-earners are required to maintain even a modest standard of living. Hence women have become providers of turkey products, tofu hotdogs, and assorted bacon equivalents. Without this in any way easing man's burden, it has added to the woman's, thereby jostling around the markers where men and women traditionally stood. For many, life has become a navigational nightmare.

In olden days, a man could point to the roof over the family dwelling and proudly exclaim, "I built that!" Now, he is lucky if he can maintain it in good-enough shape to keep out the rain. Not only hasn't he built anything of value in the home, but he cannot even claim the satisfaction of a job well done in the workplace. Jobs have become so specialized that seldom does one individual see the rewards of his handiwork, from inception to the final product. Whether we make brooms for a living, write software, or design buildings, like Charlie Chaplin in *Modern Times*, we are reduced to tightening bolts on a faceless machine. Increasingly, in most pursuits, specialization has cost us the pride of accomplishment.

I'm not convinced in the slightest that modern man has evolved to become a cog in an industrial wheel. As men feel and act devalued, they become both suspect and suspicious. The old ways, the ways of their fathers, are obviously not appreciated anymore. A family man who would have earned the Good Housekeeping Seal of Approval in the fifties would now be stamped "reject." Thus, when Dad comes home at night, in addition to bacon he unpacks frustration, fear, fatigue, conflict, and confusion. The effect becomes even more pernicious. As a man loses self-respect, he gradually loses the respect of the family. It's an everyday fact in thousands of households.

One of my greatest joys as a father was my daily re-entry, when my first two daughters were little. They received me at the door like bouncing basketballs, with their overflowing happiness to see me. We would roll on the grass or on the carpet, enjoying life's moment to the hilt. When I left for work in the morning, whenever possible, my wife would hold the two little ones to the window to wave their daddy goodbye.

More recently, I've been in houses where Dad comes home totally unacknowledged by wife or children. Only the old mutt drags itself tail-wagging to the door. I think this is a tragic development that sums up the tensions in families today. Naturally, if you persist in coming home as an absolute grouch, nobody will be glad to see you. This is one vicious cycle.

Clearly, if it progresses to the point that you begin to avoid coming home altogether, you are in imminent danger of becoming an absent father. If this is where you find yourself today, I urge you to see a counselor before you commit to a course of action that will change the lives of several people, most of all that of your child, who almost certainly will be adversely affected.

What can you do to decompress before descending upon your family with the full weight of your darkness? I can tell you what won't work: pouring a double martini, with or without your wife's participation. This is the so-called arsenic hour, the time between arriving home and sitting down to dinner, when all devilish plans foment.

What I find useful is to take a bit of time for myself. I greet my family as warmly as I can, and tell them that I'll be back in a few minutes. This of course requires in-advance negotiation with your partner, or she might not take kindly to what might appear as pampering yourself while she is knee deep in doo-doo. I have a stationary bike in one room where I work myself into a sweat. A half hour of this rids me of most of the devil. Then, a shower and a change of clothing into something loose and comfortable, and I'm back to my adorable self, gung-ho to participate.

Now, I know I'm describing an idealized middle-class set-up. It may be that your partner isn't home yet and you have to pick up the child from day care. There are a million different situations. All I'm saying is that vigorous exercise, after a long stretch of sitting at the job, is helpful in relieving frustration and safeguarding you from conflict.

If you have a place to retreat at work, stay behind for a minute and reflect on what's happening at home. Or take a short walk. Whose birthday party is Susie invited to? What have you been asked to pick up on the way home? Ah, the plumber was there to fix the kitchen sink, so dinner might not be ready on time. When you feel settled and have a reasonable expectation that you're not walking onto any landmine surprises, lean back and close your eyes. (I know, the rush hour! Must get going.)

I also try to make sure that our evenings have a balance: time for the kid, time for you and your partner alone together, and a time for you and your partner alone separately. Family life is such a challenge that you can never let it take care of itself. There's always a need for prevention—to examine and diagnose before trouble erupts. You may think that two people who love each other should be able to get along by doing what comes naturally. Alas, it is seldom so. There are traps at every turn. As much as you need to be a conscious parent, you need to be a conscious partner.

CHAPTER 7

BUOYANT IN TROUBLED WATERS

One of the bigger challenges of fathering is not losing sight of your partner. Your best attempts can be foiled if you fail to devote as much attention to your partner as you do to your baby. From day one. Which means, always, and especially after that fateful roll in the hay. The perky, full-of-fun, easygoing, and generous woman you used to know may become temporarily unavailable. More than you ever imagined, you may find a moody, whiny, aggressive, and generally pain-in-the-butt impostor claiming squatter's right on your partner's body. You have heard about midnight cravings for pickles and strawberry shortcake. What you haven't heard is that by the time you're back with the goods she'll be fast asleep, has changed her mind, or is ready to chew you out for taking too long.

She's out of sorts because of nausea, constipation, hemorrhoids, depression, and anxiety, among others, and yes, she may be suddenly prone to tantrums. You have been told, and you have no problem believing it, that the culprit is the hormone devil. If only you had access to an exorcist! At this point, you may begin wondering what you got yourself into.

Or you may be one of the lucky ones. Your partner may carry her pregnancy like a new dress, ride even-keeled through the whole enterprise: no mood swings, no energy fluctuations, and no change in body image. But don't gloat; you're not out of the woods yet. There's still that minor detail of the delivery.

You have rehearsed it dozens of times, every possible scenario and remedial measures should anything go wrong. You can do the whole thing in your sleep. Good, because it will likely happen at three A.M.

You are going through the first stage of labor and it's all ticking like a Swiss watch. She is on top of her contractions because she has done all that Lamaze and because you are there with her, her support system and confident coach.

WHOA! What happened here? Is she really screaming for me to get the fuck out of her life, that she never wants to see me again? That it's all my fault that she has to go through this?

Naturally, you're devastated. In an instant, she totally loses interest in you, as if you were a ceiling tile, and focuses all her attention on God, the attending physician. Only He can take away the pain!

Now, she's lost interest in the doctor and effusively begs you to come and hold her hand. She needs you and has never loved you more than at this moment. But she informs you straight-faced that she's changed her mind. She's not going to have the baby today and wants you to take her home. NOW!

And with the next contraction she grabs your thumb and proceeds to twist it like the green top off a radish. Thank God, you have completed your course in Zen meditation for self-control. It would never do for the father to do the screaming during delivery.

The next day, you take mother and child home. But it's a different woman than you've known to date. Unless you luck out on this one too, postpartum letdown may begin to blanket your home. And it comes with frequent episodes of inconsolable tears and feelings of loss of purpose. Not even the gorgeous little tyke in the crib can make her smile for more than a few seconds. She can't sleep and she hurts all over. And she is not shy about passing this along.

"Where the hell have you been? You leave me when I need you most. Is this the kind of father you plan to be?" "But honey, you asked me to get some fruit," you reason, lamely. You feel crushed and pessimistic. She's become a stranger, and not a likeable one at that. Nothing you do is good enough.

This is where you face your *real* personality test. This is where you're called upon to extend yourself 500 percent. And don't count on any encouragement, certainly not from your spouse. This is the loneliest part of the journey, and you must keep reminding yourself that it won't last forever. The experience of overcoming this tribulation will stand you in good stead.

A reality check is in order. Remember, this woman who is presently indisposed will be once again the woman you fell in love with. Of all the possible men she has ever met, she had chosen you to be the father of her baby. There is no greater gift a woman can give a man. Under the haze there's a gallant heart beating forward to rejoin you in due course.

On the positive side, more of baby care will fall on your shoulders, which serves to accelerate your bonding. If you're wise, you will continue with your participation when the storm clouds eventually pass. Your partner will remember and appreciate your capacity and generosity of being loving when she was unlovable even in her own eyes.

As bad as it may have seemed in the midst of her pregnancy, there were nights to remember fondly. Admit it. Occasionally, when she was asleep, exhausted and at peace with you and the universe, you watched her angelic face and you fell in love all over again. You put your hand on her belly and whispered to your kid to hang in there. Mom will be okay—we'll just have to give her time. When morning came, she smiled and held you to her body, as close as your baby allowed, and all was well with the world. Off you went to work, with optimism in your smile, knowing that the day would be just fine.

There are certain temptations to be on the lookout for. One is to regress into childlike neediness. This is one time when you'll have to make a conscious decision to derive satisfaction merely from a job well done in the home. There will be few perks, just a lot of hard work. Another is the sudden realization that there are other women out there and that some of them are giving you the eye. A lot of men have strayed during this phase, lacking the inner fortitude to tough it out. Don't become a casualty.

In short, put your partner ahead of yourself. Love and cherish her like never before. Mostly, trust her. She'll be back sooner than you think.

CHAPTER 8

HAVE A LIFE
(YOU'VE ALWAYS HAD ONE)

A pediatrician with many children of his own had this piece of wisdom to pass on to us when we were expecting our first child: "You've obviously fashioned a life for yourselves you both enjoy, that you're comfortable with. You go out, you entertain, you travel, you watch TV, you listen to music. Where babies come from there was none of that. If you ask me, or even if you don't, my advice is to make the baby adjust to what you already have rather than trying to fit yourselves like some pretzel into a new fairyland existence that never was and you could never maintain for any length of time."

Luckily, we heeded his advice. In fact, his words have been an inspiration with each of my subsequent kids.

We have all had the experience of walking into some households where the parents are cowering in silence and darkness—no stereo, no TV, conversation if any carried on in whispers. You'd think somebody died. "Our baby is such a light sleeper, the slightest noise wakes him up. You know how it is." Well, yes and no. I know enough to know that it doesn't have to be like that.

Kids have been exposed to the sounds of human traffic from the day they were dropped into this world and will sleep through anything. Many children, myself included, have slept through the shriek of sirens and bombing raids during World War II, and not because we were somehow special. In my case, we were very poor and the four members of my family lived in a one-room apartment. Every night could have been a bombing raid as far as my sister and I were concerned and we wouldn't have been any the wiser. Life and the bombing raids did not come to a halt just because a baby had to go to sleep.

One of the many beautiful things about babies and young children is that they have no adult worries and stresses to make them insomniacs. Indeed, it is virtually impossible to keep a sleepy kid awake even if you wanted to.

I have found it useful with babies to adhere to a going-to-sleep ritual. The one my wife and I have developed from the time our children were very little went somewhat like this. For the last feed of the evening, whether nursing or on the bottle, we lowered the lights wherever we happened to be, at home or at friends, in company or alone. At the same time we began speaking to the baby in soft, soothing tones. Unnecessary stimulation, like tickling or throwing the baby up in the air, is counterproductive. A few minutes after the meal and after the last burp, one of us changed her diapers, rocked her in our arms for a while, and then put her in her crib.

You can sing to the baby if you're that way inclined, but if you do she will miss it when you're not there to do it. As the baby grows older, you can add reading a story or two, whether she can understand it yet or not. Once you develop your own ritual, you'll find it works best with determined repetition.

After the baby was safely in the crib, we returned to our ordinary lives. It's not that difficult, and if you stick to a plan, you can do it too.

When a baby's tummy is full, her pants are dry, and she's lovingly tucked in, she is at peace with the world. Especially if so are her parents. Bad vibes from frustrated, disillusioned, or otherwise needy parents create as much noise as five jackhammers. True, on occasion a sudden sound may startle Junior, but most of the time he won't even wake up enough to consciously respond. Millions of infants around the world live in tight quarters and have done so for generations, sleeping perfectly well. So can mine and yours. Ah, but there is the occasional rub.

A child may be uncomfortable for a number of reasons, the number being so large that most of the time we will never know what the exact reason might be on a given night. The chances of your partner and you agreeing on the cause will be correspondingly reduced. On occasion, nothing you do works, and you will feel driven to tearing out your hair or your partner's. If you haven't experienced it yet, let me warn you that this is one potential cesspool of parental disagreement. You each have a theory about what's the matter with the baby, what may or may not work, what should be the remedy, and surprise-surprise, your partner's conflicts with yours. And since you each feel very strongly about your views, while the screaming baby aggravates the tension by the minute, it doesn't take long to drive you at each other's throats.

In instances when nothing seems to work, consider taking the baby for a ride in the family car, which also serves to separate you from your partner. If you don't have a car, go for a walk with your baby in her buggy. If that isn't possible, do laps in the hallway of your building or in the living room.

With each child I have tried to make it easier for my wife to resume the kind of activities she was used to before her pregnancy, as soon as possible and as soon as she was physically ready. Our partner, the homebound parent, misses the whole world out there, but what she misses most of all is adult companionship. A few weeks of this kind of deprivation is sure to trigger most unpleasant consequences, when we all end up paying the price.

Babies are portable. Moreover, they fall asleep in the car. There is no need to place ourselves under house arrest. Take your partner out regularly. A change of scenery and communing with the outside world work wonders for lifting the mood. My son has seen the inside of a Chinese restaurant since he was eight. Days.

And, finally, here is what I consider the big one. At least once a week, for a few hours, revert to being the twosome you once were. Taking Saturday nights off, come flood or famine, has proven a lifesaver for my wife and me. Taking a night off seems to present a huge challenge for most young moms in the beginning, and perhaps for you as well. Something misaligned in our psyche compels us to think that a few hours of separation is akin to abandonment.

The best solution, of course, is a willing mom or mom-in-law in your geographic and emotional neighborhood. But there may not be one. And much as I hate to shock some of you, there are babysitters. If not exactly the same as handing your baby over to Satan, it sure must come a close second for many parents.

While it is true that no one can step in at a moment's notice and look after little Charlie the way you can, the good news is that he will need very little care while you're gone.

But until you are personally satisfied that your babysitter is capable and understands your baby (I'm of course taking it for granted that you have obtained references from people you trust), it's best to leave the house only after putting the baby to bed. Even then, on the first time, the sitter should arrive early enough to observe the bedtime ritual. Unless yours is an unusual case, the likelihood is that you will come home and the babysitter's biggest complaint will be that Charlie slept through the whole thing.

You may be so guilt-ridden for the first few outings, unable to converse on any other topic than your abandoned baby, that you might prematurely conclude that it's been a waste of time. But if you persevere you will eventually realize that the benefit in mental health for the two of you far outweighs the initial discomfort. Bite the babysitting bullet and take your partner out at least once a week.

CHAPTER 9

LIFE AFTER BIRTH

One of the biggest worries of an expectant father is the loss of his freedom. "Listen. Before you know it, you'll be in a shit-load of diapers. Your life will never be the same. The baby will be an albatross around your neck!" chants the cynical male.

The message hits home because of the vulnerability of the former-bachelor species, and because it sounds believable, being partly true. But just like we don't go around calling a carefully tended lawn a bed of weeds because of a few scraggly dandelions, the choice of what to focus on as fathers-to-be is ours.

How should I put it? Remember when you first fell in love? How the sky was a brilliant blue and the clouds whiter than white? How your steps were friskier and you just couldn't stop smiling? If somebody had told you before your experience of falling in love that "One day you will meet a woman who will change how you feel about everything," you might have responded, "Tell me more, I'm not sure I understand what you mean."

Having a child is a lot like falling in love, without the urgency of need. Yes, your life will change. The character of the change however cannot be explained without experiencing it first-hand. So when you hear doomsayers doing what they do best (even if some of them are voices from the bosom of your own soul), turn a deaf ear, reserve judgment, go meditate, for this is one occasion where you need to call on faith (not in the religious sense) to carry you through to the next discovery: "Aha, so that's what this is all about!"

Bringing your baby home is like having your time card stamped, heralding in your best years. The allocation of how you spend your time will certainly change. But not only by necessity. You don't want to stay away because being with the baby is so much fun. Instead of emphasizing obstacles, we can look forward to challenge and adventure and opportunity for self-renewal. One thing is for sure: nothing happens exactly the way we imagine. You'll be facing new and sometimes bewildering experiences for which life has not prepared you. So, being a father means that you have to learn it all, from A to Z, on the job. But from whom?

As I have alluded to several times in this book, there's immense support out there in the brotherhood of men, young and old. You get different things from the young than from the old. With the young, you walk side by side, exchanging tips and stories, and speak of practicalities—the day-to-day rewards and hardships of being a young father. From the men who have weathered parenting and came out confident and optimistic, you will be taking the long view: where being a parent fits into the totality of your life, and how your parenting efforts reflect the past and affect future generations. Here's where to look:

1. Seek out friends or family members who are currently expectant fathers. It helps immensely to have someone with whom to share your experiences and anxieties, as well as reinforce your positive moments. You might also come across joyful little insights you might have missed by concentrating too much on the task. And you can laugh when you find some commonality, in a way you can't right then enjoy with your partner.

2. Hopefully, you and your partner will have picked a pediatrician, keenly aware of the father experience, from whom you can ask questions regardless of how silly or trivial they may seem to you at the time.

3. Consider your dad as a support person, but only if you have a warm and empathic rapport. Keep in mind that although he means well, his primary father-child ties are with you, and it is hard for him to keep the roles distinct. A grandfather for some unknown reason is likely to be strict with you and spoil the grandchild, which makes you come out second best. For this and other reasons, most of them having to do with unfinished business, even in the warmest of families fathers and grandfathers are seldom the best mentors. But their availability, love, and masculine calm can be a source of strength in your occasional dark moment.

As information starts pouring in, whether good or bad, from various sources, there's an important distinction to keep in mind: what you hear has to do with *other* parents and *other* kids. Your child is different, as he will demonstrate on a daily basis, so do not prejudge but be prepared for entirely novel and surprising revelations.

And let us not forget an equally important source of information about your baby. Your baby. It is uncanny how much we can learn early from watching the baby really closely. Although at first his every expression is an experiment, pretty soon he learns what's appreciated. What you like and what you reward him for, your baby will give back. So in a way the baby becomes your mirror.

Your baby is also your teacher. His life is a journey, *his* journey, on which you also travel. Your appropriate place on the journey, as you will learn, is one of increasing distance with time. You cannot afford to identify with your child to the point of losing yourself. (There are lots of illustrations in this book about the perils of doing just that.) Your child's journey is not the shortest distance between two points. There are detours, false turns, and times of doubling back on distance already covered. None of this is evidence of failure; you the father have not done anything wrong. There is only trial and mastery.

So, it is true that your life will never be the same after your baby's birth. It will be richer and deeper because you'll have accepted the challenge and taken on an adventure that will draw out your dormant best.

Here's my guarantee: if you're prepared to dedicate a reasonable amount of time and energy to being a father and at the same time learn to relax about it, you'll become a perfectly good-enough father. And if you are that, watching your baby blossom will be the single most powerful feeling of accomplishment that you will ever experience.

Chapter 10

Is There Sex After Birth?

The short answer is definitely: why shouldn't there be? Your partner and you have a baby because you made love. Hopefully, because you love each other and want to go on loving each other and your child. It is safe to assume that, if your partner has had a healthy pregnancy and you've been caring, responsible, and tender, not just horny, you've made beautiful love throughout her pregnancy. That, of course, rests on the assumption that you think as I do that the pregnant female body is a gorgeously sensual and sexy gift of nature. If, on the other hand, explicitly or through insinuations, you tell her that she is fat when her body is enhanced with your child, the only sex you may have to be looking forward to is the self-service kind. If you volunteer for any job, chore, task, challenge, you will make her feel taken care of, pampered, and very much loved. My female informants tell me that during that post-delivery juncture in their lives, nothing turns them on more than that feeling of being nurtured and cherished together with their baby.

As in most matters timing is, if not everything, essential. After she's gone through the physical and emotional trauma of her life and after having stretched to and beyond limits every muscle in the southern part of her body, it will take, to be sure, some time for business to be anything near to usual. If you add into the equation exhaustion, sleep deprivation, raging hormones, and a string of other concerns, don't be surprised if having sex is not on top of her agenda. Take the cue from her. She'll come around. And she'll want to make love with you because she loves you and you'll turn her on with your exclusivity, affection, attention, and devotion. And yes, she'll be sore for awhile. You may have to be creative. Definitely not one-track-minded. What do you do in the meantime? Sleep when you can, take care of yourself, and lavish huge amounts of love on your baby—come to think of it, on your baby and her mom, too. And if you get horny, there's always you.

CHAPTER 11

TAKE A LOAD OFF YOUR BACK

"I'd do anything for my kid. He won't lack for anything. He'll never have to ask for anything; I'll anticipate his every need and desire. All I want is for him to enjoy the best life has to offer. I had nothing as a kid. Well, I won't let it happen to him—even if I have to break my back to get it for him."

Not a good idea. Breaking your back to give your kid what you never had has everything to do with you and nothing to do with your child. Your baby arrives in this world without expectations. He does not have an agenda, nor can he explain to you that he doesn't want to be saddled with yours. What he needs is air, food, a secure and safe environment, good health, lots of love, and parents who know how to laugh.

The temptation to shower our kids with every possible gadget can be enormous. I know a woman who, every time she leaves town, even for a couple of days (she is a buyer for a department store), returns with a mountain of the latest and newest gifts for her children. You can see guilt oozing from every package. She must buy her children's forgiveness because going away makes her feel less than a perfect mother, while spending hard-earned money helps atone for her sins.

The irony is that the kids only know that their mommy is away and that they miss her. When she returns they are happy. End of story. There's nothing to forgive, nor would it ever occur to them that they have been wronged in any way. On the other hand, when they see their mother plying them with gifts, they eventually sense that there's some advantage to be gained from this. Pretty soon, they start using their mother's absence to make her feel really guilty, thus gaining not only more gifts but also concessions of every kind, not because they're mean but because they're children. They didn't invent the game. Mother taught them the rules.

Early in my career as an excessively generous father, I worked three jobs so that my kids could have stylish clothes in order to live the "good life." Of course that meant nothing at all to them, but I was determined to give them what I thought was the best head start in a competitive world. So far so good. With the benefit of hindsight though, it became clear that in my case I was merely playing out the drama of giving my children what I lacked as a child.

If we give our kids all sorts of things because it satisfies some inner need, it doesn't stop with the act of giving. Like marionettes, they come home from their fancy schools, which they know we can hardly afford (because we keep reminding them in a million ways), and then perform for us. While they report on the day's events, instead of telling us what counts to them, they filter out what we're less interested in and concentrate on what we want to hear. To the extent that they are our proxies, the kids derive the greatest accolades from reciting accomplishments that we were deficient in as children, whether it be algebra, public speaking, or sports. They play out our unfinished business.

Of course no one's motivations can ever be 100 percent pure, and it makes no sense to beat up ourselves about it. But to the extent that the motives are impure, our children cannot be free to enjoy the gifts we have thrust upon them. It does not go unnoticed by them that they are somehow playing out our secret desires. This then becomes a lever for them to extract more concessions (again, because they are children), at the same time resenting their role of being puppets. Where this ends up is all around disappointment and bad karma. Not only are we breaking our backs for our kids, but they don't even appreciate it!

My second wife, Vicki, coming from an affluent family, didn't have anything to prove in the have-money-or-not department. The difference in our motivations was so startling that at first I thought she didn't really care! Later, I realized that she cared all right, but did not obsess like I did. She could stand back and enjoy seeing our kids smartly dressed or not, happy with their electronic and space age goodies or without. Her ego was not on the line. If they soiled their clothes or broke a toy, it was not the end of the world. If they liked the wrappings more than the toys, it made her laugh.

Today, I play with my child, Sacha, who is eleven, because I love her very much and also partly to heal the wounds of my own childhood. I try not to saddle her with my shtick, and for the most part I can do that because I have learned to be aware. No human being can raise children without in some part reliving his own childhood. A lot of the joy in being a parent is just that. But we do a much better job if we become aware of the army of ghosts tugging at our unconscious.

There are certain signs that warn me not to cross the line. Anytime I start getting hot under the collar about something my child did or didn't do is a pretty good indication that I am slipping into my childhood-rewrite mode. Then I have to step back and remind myself about who I am and who she is.

A friend of mine taught his daughter the alphabet with cue cards when she was only sixteen months old. She read fluently by the time she was three. He did it lovingly, and both of them got a charge out of the process. Unfortunately his wife, who had little formal schooling, used every opportunity to show off her daughter's ability to anyone who cared to pay attention. Through her child, she was trying to correct her own deficiency. The result was that the child became a show-off and shunned by her peers. When this starts early and becomes ingrained, it becomes a style that is hard to repair in adulthood.

I remember that when I was in grade school there was a quiet boy in the back of the class who never put up his hand but always knew the answers. After all the kids, hands waving, had given all the wrong answers, the teacher would zero in on the quiet boy at the back of the room. "Well, Martin, what do you think?" Martin would respond in a quiet, self-confident voice. I can't tell you the admiration I felt for that kid. Of course, I was the exact opposite. If I thought I knew the answer, no force on earth could keep me quiet in my seat.

I often wonder what happened to Martin. Did he become president of some multinational corporation, or did his repression lead him into a life of crime or more likely something totally different? Perhaps because of my childhood admiration for Martin, I've tried to instill in my children a sense of not being arrogant with their inborn gifts.

By the time my youngest, Sacha, graced our home, I had finally learned to relax a bit, not always insisting on the best and newest for her. Sacha became the first of my five children to wear hand-me-down clothes from her siblings. I now welcome secondhand books, games, bikes, and skates. In fact, Sacha and I are frequent browsers at local lawn and garage sales.

When all is said and done, your kid will much prefer to have you without a broken back and your spirit intact. There is no merit in anticipating your kid's every need and whim. If you give them everything, they'll never be able to distinguish needs from wants. Every human being needs a spiritual star to reach for, a dream he may or may not realize in his lifetime. If he is showered with material things whenever there surfaces an intangible wish or desire, he will not develop a capacity of reaching for the stars. Nor will he enjoy the reward of hard work for something real.

You and your child will both benefit from your learning to say "no." If you feel your kid's hand is constantly in your pocket, don't forget that you taught him everything he knows.

CHAPTER 12

IN AND OUT OF THE LAUNDRY BASKET

It's 2:00 A.M. You're finally just falling asleep. Until then, babe in arms, you've worn tracks into your carpet, broadloom, hardwood, linoleum, patience, and endurance. You've recited every nursery rhyme you could remember, even the one your babysitter used to sing to you in Polish. You've hummed Pachelbel's Canon so many times that you were about to collapse in a New Age trance. Nothing seemed to do any good; she just wouldn't settle down. Then miraculously, she took mercy and threw in the diaper, just as you were fantasizing putting her up for adoption or trading her in for a barkless Basenji.

Now, she is deep asleep, and you are already more asleep than awake. Your wife is oblivious to this nocturnal drama, after a sixteen- to eighteen-hour tour of maternal duty. And that was the agreement, so it's only fair. Never mind that you have to get up at 6:30. After all, you were an equal partner in deciding to have a child, not to mention an eager participant in its production.

Now you are basking with your honey on a tropical beach, just the two of you, when the howling of a siren breaks into the dream. "Where's the fire?" You bolt upright and rush to your baby's room to snatch the sleepy angel out of her cradle before the whole place goes up in flames. Ah, but it's only the little Banshee, who had second thoughts about the two of you sleeping after all.

I hate you, you little fucker! No. I take it back, I didn't mean that, please God, you didn't hear me say that. Daddy loves his little sweetheart, and louder, "Daddy loves his little sweetheart." Of course, she will be an orphan soon, because if I have to go through more nights like this, I'll either die of some obscure disease or jump off the nearest bridge.

The preceding mini-drama is not a piece of fiction. It is enacted nightly in millions of homes throughout the world. I have lived it with each of my five kids, some for just a few nights, some for months. With my youngest daughter, Sacha, I created a whole en-cyclopedia on the insomniac theme. After two months of trial and error, I succeeded in inducing her to fall asleep in her cradle. The only remaining challenge was leaving the room without making the old floorboards creak, that is, until I discovered the trick of crawl-ing away in a laundry basket.

I discovered that if I sat in a plastic laundry basket and pushed myself inch by inch on the carpet covering the old flooring, I could eventually creep out of creaking range. Necessity was the father of invention.

The good news is that, during those desperate nightly vigils, Sacha and I connected on a level beyond words. Fathers often don't hook up to young children because they don't put in the nocturnal blood, sweat, and tears. As much as sleeplessness is a curse, my daughter was signaling to me that she wanted to get to know me. She already had ample firsthand knowledge about Mom during their nine-month sojourn together, and the sixteen- to eighteen-hour days that followed, but I was an enigma and she had to make sure that I could be counted on as a reliable and worthwhile member of the team.

Sacha is eleven at the time of this writing. We've stayed very close—ours has been a seamless eleven years, to a great extent because of a healthy start based on those heroic nights. So, men facing the Night Terror, welcome it with open arms. See it as a long-term investment—a lifelong trip *with* your child, rather than as an outsider looking in.

CHAPTER 13

THE BEST DEFENSE IS NOT BEING THERE

Bullshit baffles brains . . . and new fathers. For some reason, deeply seated in the dark side of the human psyche resides the temptation of freaking out others. Should those others be particularly vulnerable, so much the better. This is acutely true on the subject of childbirth and new parenting.

A young man reports to me what his stepmother chose to share with him while his wife was pregnant: "I was on the delivery table, when suddenly I had a weird urge. 'I want a smoked pickerel and a bottle of wine or I don't deliver this baby,' I said to the nurse. She said no, and then the doctor said no—out of the question. So I crossed my legs and I held the baby in for two weeks until they finally gave me what I wanted. Then I had my daughter."

"And you're telling me this because . . ."

"Just thought you should know."

Other stories, while not as aromatic as this, succeed in grossing the daylights out of expecting fathers (and mothers, to be sure) just as effectively. Tales of men passing out in the delivery room, puking at the sight of a dilating birth canal, and so on. So what to do?

It seems part of the initiation ritual of womankind to terrify prospective parents, as if they weren't scared enough already. One woman seems to be saying to the other that regardless of how this pregnancy turns out it's nothing compared to the experience she went through. Men, not to be outdone, often relate their harrowing trip to the hospital, the red lights they had to run, the cop chase, with the baby's head almost hanging out, stopping just short of performing a Caesarean section.

My advice to pregnant parents: when a potential scaremonger leans toward you confidentially, licks his or her lips, and lowers his or her voice, then launches into his or her favorite perinatal story, interrupt decisively: "Are you about to tell me a scary, unpleasant, or morbid tale about pregnancy, labor, delivery, or early infancy? If so, I don't want to hear it. I can't afford to hear it. But if you have something positive and uplifting, I'm all ears." This should guard you against all but the most obstinate assaults.

Keep in mind that while children are conceived and carried in the same way as ever, there are also some fundamental differences between the way your parents and their parents delivered their babies. Information likely to be offered to you by someone from a previous generation is bound to be outdated, if it was ever true. Just think about all the "scientific" methods people used to predict the gender of their offspring. "She is carrying high, she is carrying low, her belly is pointed, her belly is rounded, her belly is turning purple with green polka dots." (I just threw the last in to highlight the absurdity, although the others are no less absurd.)

Equally laughable and outdated was the argument offered to me by my family physician when I expressed my wish to participate in my child's birth. "I have six kids," he pontificated, "and I was not present at the birth of any one of them. Would you want to be there for her appendectomy?" My response: "I was there for conception and through the pregnancy. It makes sense to be there for the birth—for my child's sake and my wife's sake and, most of all, for my own sake. And yes, if my wife wanted me there for her appendectomy, I'd want to be there for that too."

Deliveries are different today, due mainly to the dad's presence and participation. Most hospitals now bend over backwards to include fathers, which has tamed the whole procedure and made it less clinical.

Imagine two scenarios and then choose one that makes the most sense to you:

1. You are there throughout the whole birth, and you learn firsthand that your son or daughter has arrived and that you and your partner have come through just fine. In this scenario you see your newborn immediately. You are there when he opens his eyes for the first time, and his first view of this world will include you. You will get to hold him in your arms within minutes.

2. You do not participate in birthing. Instead, you are "down the hall," zoned out in the waiting room, or in your neighborhood watering hole. Your cell phone rings when and if somebody remembers that you too are part of the equation. By the

time you make it to the scene, they have spirited him away into a nursery awaiting future introduction. This scenario may very well set the stage of your being "down the hall" for a lot of important events in your child's life.

Quite clearly, I enthusiastically support your active involvement in all phases of your child's life, beginning with, well, the beginning. Make no mistake. Your presence makes a huge difference not only for you and your partner; it also sets the tone for your bond with your child. If you pay no attention to the horror stories and opt to participate in delivering your child, you will feel that you and your partner are a team in raising him or her from the very beginning.

No matter what those "well-intentioned" dream-stealers want to tell you, remember they are talking about themselves, often about what didn't go right for them. Your story cannot be the same as theirs because you are not them, your situation is not theirs. Your histories, your relationship, your style of facing challenges are yours, not theirs. The ill wind they blow at you only serves to unburden their load, whatever that may be. Will it all be smooth sailing? Of course not. One of the facts of life I've learned is that the unexpected tends to happen, often good and occasionally bad. What matters more than hardening yourselves to each possible eventuality is to have the resources to handle what comes up. No one has ever had your child. Your experience will be unique. There are times when we all become overwhelmed, usually in medical emergencies. But fortunately children are tough and they come through intact, if occasionally bruised.

The time to start your relationship with your child and begin shaping the new one with your partner is from the very beginning. Doing it in a collaborative, involved, and mindful way will encourage your continuing on that road forever.

CHAPTER 14

TOPSY-TURVY

At times, life is hard. But when the stork drops a new baby into your world of responsibilities, life can be damn hard. Former everyday worries gain in importance so that more of your time is given to fretting over your fears—and guess what, new ones surface all the time, real and imagined. When you consider that this new little being will be totally dependent on you and your partner, I can almost see your posture droop just a shade. Then as you think in circles about the specific burdens that shall befall you, making sure there's a roof over your head and money for formula and diapers, college education, wedding expenses, and whether you would ever have enough money to retire, your back curves a few more degrees. Perhaps you don't know this yet, and it may be just as well, but your wife's expectations of you will be quite different from what you were used to before. Moreover, her expectations will often go in the opposite directions of your preferences.

One day you come home from work exhausted, frustrated, disappointed, in short, cranky, and ready for a beer or six. You have dinner with your wife, at which you make an extraordinary effort (not being a Dustin Hoffman) to avoid betraying any hint of self-pity, e.g., "Boy, did I have the crappiest day yet!"

So, now you want to watch TV. Guess what? Your mate is feeling lonely, sad, scared, and she wants your company, affection, reassurance, courage, wisdom, strength. Since you love her and she has been through a great ordeal getting to this point, you snap to attention (perhaps not snap; let's be real—rise). She wants you to rub her back, her legs, and her tummy, but in such a manner that it shouldn't be the least suspicious of you trying to arouse her. Don't expect for a moment that the cuddle will turn into anything explosive. She is definitely not available for the saucier side of the night. So, gingerly, as if you were her father, you touch her with the purest of intention—just to make her feel relaxed and cared for. She may extend a hand in search of signs of life between your thighs, reassuring herself that she still has what it takes. That's it. You return the affection but in a way that does not turn you into a crazed satyr. She has to show you when the time is right.

Then, she needs to sleep, and so do you, but after a night of sleep, she needs to awake to face the coming day with enough good-natured energy to make the little bugger feel welcome into the household. Of course, you too need to go to work without dark circles around your eyes. If you consider your family more important than your work, guess who'll be crawling the midnight milk-detail?

That this takes a toll on you is to be expected. In fact, after a period of abstinence you may get used to the lack of sex and go into protective hibernation. Then, one night, as in the greatest sleep clichés of all times on this or any side of Hollywood, you become faintly conscious of a whimpering at your side. "What's wrong?" you ask, "Are you crying, baby?"

"You don't make love to me anymore," she sobs. "I'm fat and ugly."

"That's not true," you protest, and try to explain how you have been dying to do just that but you were holding off because you thought she wasn't ready.

The long and the short of it is that you and she are destined to be out of synch for the next little while regardless of what you do or do not do, as you both gradually mold into your new lifestyle. Pregnancy, childbirth, and life after birth culminate in a powerful whirlwind for many women. Woe to the man who is either unprepared or unwilling to empathize with and validate his partner's topsy-turvy existence.

These are trying times for you, the bewildered father, and can make you vulnerable to the preying singles, booze, and married singles. Women who have been lusting for your charms know your vulnerability and are willing to become shoulders to lean on and the easy progression to below shoulders. You are aching for undivided love, to be titillated, to be understood, all things that your mate is unable to provide. I have known too many men in my counseling career who fell ignominiously in this period.

One client, Sam, landed in the Venus Trap a short month after his wife delivered their son. The first step on this steep and rocky road, by his personal account, was preceded by gut-wrenching moral agonizing. But soon it became easier. "For a little while," he reported, "I thought I found the perfect solution. Then it started to get complicated." Monique, his mistress, fell in love. As intoxicating as this felt, Sam began to feel an icy breeze on his naked back. Monique began to make demands and as he tried to pull away he discovered he could not. There were painful crying scenes that Sam found intolerable on his conscience already burdened by guilt.

His reasoning was becoming clouded. Monique being totally focused on him displayed exactly those qualities he yearned for. Of course that was not all of Monique, just the components he was missing in his wife, not something that he was aware of. He began to imagine a life with Monique, carefree, titillating, without much responsibility, languid amorous nights with a much younger woman—no loose skin, no flab, no stretch marks. In other words, he allowed himself to believe that his affair with Monique was an act of fate, an encounter with his soul mate, and that it was meant to be. He was in love with two women, he thought. So what was wrong with that? It took six weeks for him to pack up and leave his wife and son, "temporarily," to find out how he really felt.

Then, chaos. His conscience prevented him from truly enjoying himself. It made him darker and darker and consequently a lot less lovable than in the romance-inspired relationship that Monique had bargained for. Eventually, he came to the realization that he did not love Monique after all and that, even if he had, the love would wither away in the shadow of his guilt, shame, and sadness over the abandonment of wife and child. Unfortunately for him, his wife felt so deeply betrayed that she was not willing to even consider reconciliation. At this writing, she is re-evaluating.

In a show of good faith, Sam broke off all contact with Monique. Now, he has two women he has hurt and who don't trust him.

He acknowledges that if he had to do it all over he would seek out his more soulful male friends for companionship, and to allay the sexual noises in his head he would work them off in a gym or running in the ravines near his house. He had taken a dangerous detour but he is convinced that he is now definitely on track, if only his wife will take him back. He is hanging in.

Chapter 15

It's Always Darkest Before
It's Totally Black

"All my youth, I dreamed about getting married and becoming a dad," Hal, a new member with only two sessions under his belt, stated one Wednesday night in a men's group I've been leading for fifteen years. "My version of the future went along the lines of a sitcom."

Hal was in his early forties, a real estate lawyer and fiction writer, married for the second time, with four kids, two per partner. "I lost my mom very early, and to all intents and purposes I also lost my dad. After she died, Dad never regained his energy as a parent, let alone the energy or desire to make a single-parent family thrive. I was mostly raised by my friends' parents and the occasional aunt who came by to visit. All through my teens I kept reminding myself that whatever happens, I will never do this to *my* kids. Whether it was drowning them in silence," Hal continued, "invisibility, depression or mistrust, unrealistic (and at times, unreal) expectations, or the ever-present 'This is so because I am your father' or 'You'll do as I say because I am your father.'

"Around fourteen, my life took a dramatic turn. I became a good football player and gained a lot of self-confidence, not to mention girlfriends. Eventually, step by step, my father could no longer control me. All this is to say that whatever I learned about fathers I learned from my dad. It can be summed up as: 'Just do the opposite of what he did.' The amazing thing is that having a sad and lonely childhood did not sour me on having a family. Quite the contrary. I had resolved to have many children and to raise them properly, like I should have been raised.

"Flash forward twelve years. A year after we were married, my wife announced that she was pregnant. I was on top of the world. The prospect of starting a family filled me with tremendous joy. The pregnancy was going splendidly. No morning sickness, no fatigue, no mood swings, no cravings. Just a baby doing her thing and the two of us loving every minute of it.

"In the eighth month my wife developed toxemia. The doctor sent her to bed. Soon she became depressed, anxious, and crabby beyond words. I had to work, go to school, shop, cook, do laundry, and be a smiling, supportive partner. Just to make matters worse, because I was perpetually tired I lost my part-time job. Now we had financial problems.

"Then, one day, it hit home. Holy shit. This is what life is going to be like from here on. Busting my ass, living from paycheck to paycheck, using up my student loan, no time for anything to further my career. And I was scared out of my wits for my wife and child. Some sitcom this life was turning out to be. I saw myself becoming the living cliché, 'Be careful what you wish for.'

"I was feeling sorry for myself and maybe I was justified. I took to walking after dinner, only it was more like rushing to deliver an urgent message. One summer night, the night before my wife was to be induced at thirty-two weeks, I noticed this older man walking behind me. When I picked up the pace so did he. We were forced to a stop at a red light. 'You're quite a walker,' he said, without a sign of being out of breath. 'I've never seen a Canadian walk like you. You must either be a foreigner or in a lot of pain.'

"I wanted to tell him to fuck off, but his eyes were gentle and I had the impression that he cared. Suddenly I became a little boy and all I wanted to do was cry.

"'Let me buy you a cup of coffee,' he said.

"I shook my head, afraid to speak because I knew my voice would break. We sat on a bench on the corner of Bloor and St. George. The sun had set and I felt anonymous enough not to be recognized.

"'You must be wondering,' the man said, 'so maybe I should tell you who I am, or rather what I do, since what I do is not who I am. I taught high school for forty years. Since I retired, I have been volunteering wherever I was needed and lately at the Downtown Distress Center. Believe me, I've learned to recognize a person on the edge. If you want to talk, I'm here to listen.'

"We spoke, or rather I spoke and he listened, for I don't know how long. I told him the story of my life, including some details I've never shared with anyone, like when my father stomped on my train for accidentally dropping my late mother's favorite vase.

God, did I hate him for that! I was six.

"He looked at me for a full minute without saying a word. Then he smiled sadly and said, 'What parents do to their children . . . with the best of intentions.'

"'You're not talking about my father, the bastard who ruined my life. Best of intentions?'

"'What are you, twenty-six, twenty-seven? You just started a family. You're in love with your wife. She is the perfect woman for you, and there will never be another like her. Then she dies. You're left with a two-year-old son. You're out of a job. You become depressed. You're sapped of all energy and hope. You get one menial job after another. You cannot get ahead because you have a young child to look after, which is the only thing keeping you from taking your life. Let me ask you this. What kind of a father do you think *you* would make? Here, let me give you my card. Call anytime.' He stood up and walked away, without glancing back.

"I sat on the bench sobbing like a kid until midnight."

Nobody in the group spoke. Some were clearing their throats.

"Hal," I said, when the time seemed right. "Thank you for letting us in. It was a heartfelt story. I felt sad listening to you telling it. You may want to ask the guys what effect it had on them."

"I take it your wife and your baby came out okay?" asked Kevin, one of the members of the group.

"Yes, thank God."

"And you and your wife?"

"We were pretty solid after that. I can thank the teacher for that. We met many times. He even showed up at St. Mike's when my wife was being induced. I hadn't remembered mentioning the hospital, but I must have."

"He sounds like a biblical character," said Paul. "You sure you didn't dream him up?"

"Or a mentor," said Kevin. "André always speaks in mystical tones about mentors. A parent could never do that, get up, and leave without a word."

"He left with impact," said Marty, "leaving him to sort things out. He had no personal investment. He just wanted to help."

"Don't forget wisdom," said Kevin. "Could you see yourself as a mentor?"

"Not right now. Right now I need a mentor."

"We all do," I said.

CHAPTER 16

IS THERE A FATHER IN THE HOUSE?

If you spend time with your infant consistently, without your partner present, she will learn to identify your voice very early. Experience as well as research has shown that the lower register, male voice will help a fretful child settle down faster than a higher register, female voice. If you spend daily time with your baby, she'll recognize you and will reward your presence with a smile. I can tell you from experience that, when you see that smile beaming directly at you, you will feel one with the world. What happens next? You become addicted to that smile and will need your regular fix. More than that. Your child's acknowledgment of you and her appreciative feedback will reinforce your sense of competence. Remember those long-ago moments when you were scared to hold her for fear of dropping her? By the time your appearance summons a smile across her face, those will be distant memories.

Now, if you're prepared to enhance your commitment with a (big) bag of patience, tolerance, and a spirit of child-centeredness, you'll have created the foundation upon which your relationship can build. Helping you on your way will be an endlessly evolving curiosity and pleasure. But for this to happen, you have to be the parent in charge often enough for you to see yourself (and to be perceived) as a driving force. Such a hands-on, interactive parent would never consider spending time as babysitting. That's a job for which we pay an outsider. Fathering is a mission.

Here are some suggestions about what constitutes hands-on fathering:

A) Always plan ahead. Think what preparation is required for your child's needs to be met. If you take your toddler to a jamboree and she has a bruiser of a bowel movement, be prepared to produce at least one diaper and the necessary cleansing products from the diaper bag that *you* have packed. "Can I bum a diaper from you?" addressed to a mom next to you is poor form. "And while you're at it, lend me a wipe, some powder, and a jar of baby cream, if you will." These are clear instances of inadequate foresight and caring.

B) None of this amounts to a hill of beans if you're not factoring into your busy schedule a slot for spending with your child, giving it at least as much weight as you would for a sales meeting, doctor's appointment, equipment safety inspection, tennis game, or romantic date with your partner. Don't improvise in the last minute and settle for fifteen hurried minutes while your mind is elsewhere. If you see this as a chore, akin to putting out the garbage or doing the laundry, you are already behind the eight ball. This is a main event, not a side show. Needless to say, and consider this a fringe benefit, you will grow more gallant and desirable in your partner's eyes than if you'd been candy-dipped in pheromones. Nothing is a greater turn-on for Mom than seeing her funsome leading man enjoying her offspring.

C) This is rather basic, but as my late mentor Jorge Rosner used to say (twenty-five years ago), "Spell out the obvious. What's obvious to you may not be obvious to others." Make your material contribution to the family coffers generously and unselfishly. Don't expect her to take on a task so that you have one fewer, unless it is in the spirit of fair barter (see below).

D) Participate in all decisions and in all phases of your child's life from the earliest beginnings. In matters such as the choice of physician or midwife, the kind of birthing, childbirth education, hospital or home delivery, breastfeeding or formula, the times family and friends can see the baby and a myriad other decisions, don't just shrug your shoulders, passively shirking your contribution. If you opt for co-op daycare, make sure you too put in your time. If you enroll your child in activities, participate in them. Take your share of driving, car pooling, shopping for baby clothes and toys. Go with your partner to all doctor appointments and attend every one of your child's performances in class. Participate in planning and hosting your kid's birthday parties. Take her to friends' houses and get to know the parents. Help coordinate playtimes. In short, be regularly involved in all the minutiae we fathers tend to relegate to (dump on) our partners.

The Industrial Revolution has chased, if not banished, us from much of our children's lives. Now, it is trying to do the same to mothers, as the necessity of two full incomes drives children into the arms of third-party caregivers. The Fathering Revolution is bringing us a bit closer to equal footing but is still far from where we should be.

If you didn't get much fathering in your childhood, you probably can't even imagine what it's all about. My intention in writing this book is to make you familiar with the concept in time, if possible even before your child is born. By the time you have finished this book you'll know what you missed or didn't miss in your childhood. Now that you know, you are in a position to provide it to your child, and indirectly to yourself. Everybody wins.

For the most part, if you've had happy memories with your dad, your child will have similar memories. In my case, the opposite was true. All along, I knew what I was missing and took silent oaths not to deprive my children when the time came. Later, as I was putting my oaths into practice I began to feel the healing power of empathic fathering. I became a good-enough father. And by now you may have learned that good enough is good enough . . . most of the time.

E) Be a mindful, collaborative, and assertive partner—in other words, pull your weight as equally as possible. Make sure that through your efforts your partner sees you as an equal, not a cartoon father, nodding "Yes, dear," at every opportunity. In too many households moms lapse into the role of the primary parent through dads' defaulting. At times, they love it. But at others they resent and even hate it, and sometimes they do both at the same time. Too many fathers complain that they're auxiliary or secondary parents, not consulted about or enlisted in the most important aspects of the child's life. They see themselves as money bags, and resent it immensely. I've heard many principal breadwinners complain over the years that the only way they can exert any authority is by withholding dough. If you find yourself in this reality, you've participated in formulating it. If you are drifting in that direction, this is the time to sit down, as often as needed, to articulate a full participatory democracy with equal rights and responsibilities. And then make sure that you live up to your end of it. If this ailing family picture is already in place, think of remedial actions and write them down, along these lines:

1. What's important to me? What are the non-negotiable things I must have and those I cannot abide?

2. Now that I know what I want and don't want, what am I prepared to change, give up, sacrifice, or barter to make this happen?

3. When all the above is done, I must create with my partner a schedule for phasing in each action.

This will be a learning process, much of it trial and error, with detours and roadblocks, so that it soon becomes clear that this is an evolutionary task. If the two of you are truly committed to the plan, there can be no failure—only attempts at mastery. Just as when your child stumbles and falls while learning to take her first steps, you don't throw up your hands and lament, "This kid will never walk; we may as well give up." Concentrate on the accomplishment and not the shortcoming of your plan. Tomorrow is another day to fix what went wrong and fine-tune what went right.

CHAPTER 17

THE VANISHING ACT

Randy took a good look at his wife perhaps for the first time since the so far eight-hour labor ordeal had started. He saw the determination in her scrunched-up face to push out her child as soon as possible, and beyond, the unmistakable expression of pain and fear, perhaps the scariest sensation of the whole event. The twenty-five-year-old Randy, barely older than a child, and about to embark on *the* personal challenge of his life, was shaken by a chilling shiver.

Petra, for the first time in their five-year marriage, longed for a transfusion of some of Randy's male fighting spirit. But she could also sense what was happening to him. He was frightened out of his wits.

She and she alone could usher this baby out of her uterus and into the world. But she wanted his participation and it was quickly clear that he had little to give. Not that she hadn't had advance warning. Randy was strangely unavailable for her prenatal classes, whatever the appointment time she would choose. Instead, his mother, Heather, accompanied her and became her coach.

Heather, a cabdriver by occupation, had assisted in delivering three children in her career. Now, she was at the bedside, holding out her hand as if in proxy for her son. They had never spoken about his squeamishness or whatever you would call it. Emergencies of any kind would cause him to bolt into the farthest corner of the apartment, or out of Dodge in the worst case. He turned pale at the sight of a Band-Aid.

"You're doing splendidly, sweetheart, couldn't be doing any better," said Heather. "You're doing better than I ever did. I'm proud of you. It won't be much longer, I'm sure."

Randy saw what was happening from his shadowy station behind his mother. He knew that he was making himself utterly superfluous. But as much as he wanted to be supportive, affectionate, and master of his own domain, everything worked against him. Instead of conquering his weakness, he felt himself being driven further and further into remoteness, into a deep fog of sadness and impotence.

And the escape lay in anger. "I knew if my mother came she would squeeze me out," he reasoned. "This is my baby, too. What business does she have horning in like this? She's here because she thought I wouldn't come through, that I was a good-for-nothing. She's made me into an intruder." With that, he turned and without a word dashed out of the delivery room.

After a couple of hours, roaming through the field of golden barley and maize, in the waning days of summer, the realization slowly came to him that there was only one person to blame. The prenatal classes, his squeamishness, his nonactions in emergencies. Maybe he *was* a good-for-nothing, and Petra, always the stronger and wiser, deserved something better, someone better. Instead of rushing back to the hospital, now shame kept him away.

As for Petra, she thought her husband felt sick to his stomach and had run out to throw up. It wouldn't have been the first time. But, after it was all over and Dahlia was born, there was still no sign of him and she became concerned. Maybe he'd fainted. But Heather knew better. "Don't worry. I'll bring him back," she said.

Randy was disconsolate. What a mess he had made of things! With this kind of a start, what kind of a father would he be? He began to sense that not only the act of delivery but also the fear of becoming a father had driven him to bolt. His own father had chosen the exit route when Randy was five and he had never seen him since. Did the idea of running away come from his father? He didn't have any friends who would have understood any of this, so there was no one to turn to.

By now, he was unconsciously heading toward his secret spot on the shores of Granite Lake, a little hollow at the bottom of the rock face he had discovered many years ago. He lay down on the sand, curled up into a ball, and hoped that the tears would come and bring relief, like they used to when he was a child.

"Come on boy, let's go to your wife and baby, they need you," he heard Heather's voice as if in a dream. But Heather was there in flesh and blood. "It will all work out, you'll see."

"I feel so awful, " he said as they were driving back to the hospital. "What will she think of me?"

"Just say to her what you just told me."

Which he did, and Petra forgave him, happy to have her new family together for the first time. "Just hold our baby and hold me. We'll work this out. I need you and I love you."

"I feel so worthless. I'm always thinking you'll leave me."

"Listen. No one expects you to be a super-dad overnight. I know your childhood and you'll have plenty of time. I'll never leave you."

Had Randy had a decent, trustworthy group of friends, men who have faced the challenge and have come out victorious from the encounter, he would likely not have panicked. As a man, he was cruising alone in uncharted waters, without a support system to give him courage. Randy and Petra had a lot of work ahead of them. Life as they knew it was going to change.

Randy, first do the things that matter most to the family and to your child, which means that some of your evenings out with the boys will have to be demoted on the list. This may sound like a disaster at first glance, but if you want to make a go of it, and if you want your child for life, you'll have to make a conscious decision to defer gratification. This is not intuitive to every father (or mother) but after a year or two of conscious effort there will be enough warm radiance in your home that it will overshadow all you think you have given up. Do not sink into martyrdom. Well, okay, for a day or two. Do not neglect your present pastimes entirely. As you and your family mature into cohesiveness, you will find your natural balance.

And another thing. Much of you is still a child. It happens. Not every part of us matures at the same rate. I feel you are terrified at closing the book on childhood, something that you'll not be aware of because this type of introspection has yet to mature in you. So far, sudden parenthood (because you haven't really faced up to it until today) has been a disaster. But soon you will discover the sublime pleasure of a successful burp, expertly executed by holding her just right, and tapping at just the right spot with just the right rhythm. Then you watch her puzzled little face: "Did that come from me? Gee, wow. I'm good, ain't I?"

Randy, if you read this you'll recognize your story although I have made changes so that others will not. I hope you have taken my advice on obtaining counseling and that you'd found it useful in coming to terms with your dad. I had only seen you once, three years ago, when you accompanied your mother to one of her last sessions in my office. Just give your marriage a chance. Give fatherhood a chance. We don't like being inadequate at anything. We think we have to be the best. Well, if you make it your priority to become really proficient at it, you'll be a good-enough father. At times—many times—you're bound to screw up. Be thrilled with your successes and don't dwell on the mistakes. Thank you, Randy. Your story was one of the reasons I was inspired to write this book for all the young men for whom becoming a father is a terrifying experience.

CHAPTER 18

WHERE IS POPPA?

Hardly a day goes by that I don't hear some hair-raising story about an individual who was mistreated by his father. I also have clients who would give an arm and a leg to have been mistreated by their fathers. They would have preferred it, or so they imagine, to the incessant pain or numbness of the absence of their fathers in their childhood. An abusive father as well as absent fathers can create havoc with children's lives, lasting for many, many years, if not forever.

I too have a hole in the core of my being (located in a well-defined area around the solar plexus) that my father left as his legacy. For the first eight years of my life, when life was still more or less normal in Hungary, my father was already a less than visible presence. I remember an assignment in elementary school where we had to draw a sketch of our fathers. My picture was a spread-out newspaper, with fingers holding it on each side. He spent most days sunk deep into a worn-out, comfortable armchair.

He was not a bad man. Far from it. I think if our apartment house were burning down he would have risked his life to save me. On some remote level, I took it for granted that he loved me. And because he also took it for granted, he never had to think about it or had the need to show it.

This is a very common problem for us fathers, where under the best of circumstances we have so little time for the little tyke, just as we have very little time for anything else in our lives. When taken to task by our partner, with a "You don't spend much time with the kids—they'll end up thinking you don't love them," we tend to respond with a "How can you think that? I'm busting my ass 24/7. That's not proof enough how much I love them? The ungrateful little bastards."

I don't know how to break the news to you, comrades, but it is no longer enough for us to grunt upon entering our abode, secure in those deep and silent emanations of our love. We may be exceptional providers and devoted mates and dads, and most of us come straight home with the bacon, and we don't stay out nights carousing or gambling. But these things are no longer enough. They are not enough for our mates and certainly not enough for our children. What it boils down to is this: if you want to bring up healthy children you actually have to put in the time. And it's not only sporadically, now and then. Just think of your child silently asking every day, "What have you done for me lately?"

When my mother went into labor, my father was sent out to the courtyard to cool his heels. Only hours later did he find out that he'd had a son. Of course it would have been unheard of for him to take the next day off; he would've been instantly fired.

From the very beginning, it was made perfectly clear to him that his rightful place was at arm's length from his child. It's what was expected. Every night, when he arrived home exhausted, he did what came naturally: sink into his chair and wait for supper to be served. It's what was expected. My father, as I said, was not a bad man. Nor was he a particularly good man. Whatever sort of man he was, he wasn't there.

We need to resolve to be involved with our kids in all phases of their lives. If need be, let us schedule time for our child as we would with an important client, or a meeting with our boss, or watching the Super Bowl. Spending time with our kid is much more important than filing income tax returns. Both cost money, but our child will be an important part of our lives long after we stop paying taxes.

Sure, there is something mind-numbing about sitting on the floor sorting out blocks of wood with a two-year-old. Hardly have you finished when you can begin again. Kids love repetition. They like the same stories read to them night after night. They love ritual. Maybe their food has to be cut up just so. And they refuse to sit in a high chair. It's enough to drive you insane and throw up your hands: "Let Mom handle it."

But the investment in time is an infusion of your love. You're doing it for your child because you love him. And the earlier you begin the better it gets. Soon you will realize you're no longer doing it for him but for your own enjoyment. Don't make "Daddy, I hardly knew you" your kid's favorite song.

Make sure that you take part in the big events of your child's life. And here's the rub: *all* events are important. If you were down the hall when she was born, at the pub when she sat up for the first time, at a poker game with the boys when she takes her first steps, if you just happen to be out, maybe trying to make a decent living when she is learning to swim, skate, ride the bike, draw her first stick-figure, fix the tire, bake an apple pie, laugh and cry without your presence as participant or witness, then you're an absent father. When your child experiences these things in your absence, you gradually become a stranger in her eyes. And you begin to feel estranged yourself. One day you wake up with a bitter taste and the words in your mouth: "I'm nothing but a checkbook." Who's responsible for that, my friend? Whose idea was it to give them everything money can buy? Including a hole in their heart where Dad used to be?

Remember, whether you're there or not there, your son will do his best to be just like you. And if he tries to be the opposite, he'll likely fail. To absorb you into his makeup is hard-wired into his brain. Your daughter will look for a male partner just like you, her dad. If you were not there, she'll pick someone likely to be absent a lot just like you.

Once you become aware of how important you are to your child and remind yourself of this fact several times each day, you cannot help but become a conscious parent. Your being absent will become the exception rather than the rule. And good habits feed on themselves. You'll come to realize that you're doing a great job. And what a satisfaction that is!

CHAPTER 19

KRAMER VS. KRAMER REVISITED

One of the most poignant movies I have ever seen about fathers stepping up to the plate, striking out a few times, then hitting a grand slam is *Kramer vs. Kramer*. Dustin Hoffman's character, a bit of a workaholic, is caught in the trap of upward mobility: striving for personal satisfaction through success at work. One night, he comes home to his luxurious Manhattan apartment ready to give his wife his career-related good news before even hugging his little boy. Instead of a standing ovation, what waits for him is the stark revelation that no news about work can be good enough for his wife since she's about to leave him anyway, as well as their child. She is not leaving him for another man but for a woman—herself.

Meryl Streep does such a great job of portraying a self-absorbed wife who places her need to discover herself above all else that just about every man who has seen the movie is ready to spit fire when recalling her character. Dustin Hoffman, on the other hand, draws nothing but admiration. We swell with pride contemplating the quality of nurture a father can deliver if only he will put his mind to it.

On deeper reflection, I struggle with the scenario. Yes, I am thrilled that a man with complete lack of experience in fathering (in this case self-inflicted) demonstrates with great credibility that a father can reach deep and pull out what it takes—that father's milk is real. But then I wonder how any man could have let himself sink so low as to (a) have no clue about how to make breakfast, and (b) fly into a full-blown tantrum in front of his bewildered little boy who's already minus one parent and can't make sense of the second.

There are scenes where one cannot empathize with the father, where the kid's view of his father and his new world becomes frightening and overwhelming. The boy is clearly showing that nothing is well in his universe. Instead of dropping everything else and taking time off from work, Dad stays overstressed. The boy, instead of getting tender loving care, is pummeled by his father's wrath.

Yet, thanks to Hoffman's acting skills, even at his worst the father is not unredeemable. One can only imagine the father's own upbringing that encouraged him to become self-centered and focused exclusively on professional success. He became the Great Master, while his son and wife were relegated to satellite status, with their rich Manhattan address, private school, grand lifestyle, and expensive home furnishings. Once he is forced to realize that he is after all master of his own destiny, he adjusts his values, sacrificing a few notches on the career ladder.

What's regrettable is that it takes this type of crisis for a man to stop and ask himself: "What's important? What do I have to change, give up, risk, or sacrifice to live by what's important?" But parenting was his wife's role. She had to fly the coop before he could understand his real values and act accordingly.

Some men in his situation (too many) would have run out the front door without looking back. Others would have drafted their parents or a sister to look after the child or hired a housekeeper. Kramer, on the other hand, does the truly manly thing. He rises to the occasion and does what must be done and the way it must be done.

After the wife decides that she has been gone long enough and that she's found herself, she returns asking for her child back. Of course she does. She is his mom no matter what. But by then, as my wife remarked, dad has become mom too.

A bit sad, I'd say. When a father is aloof, an adjunct parent, an also-ran, he's seen as a typical father. When he's right in the thick of things, he's a mother.

I've a client named Ron, a carpenter by trade, a stay-at-home dad, and homemaker by mutual agreement. His wife is in a profession where she earns more than her husband would in his trade. When asked to comment honestly about the experience, he has difficulty admitting how hard it is, how he finds little to enlighten and brighten his day when the work is done, and that it is never really done. To make things even less tolerable, he is the constant target of not so benevolent ribbing by the other homemakers in his street. "So what do I do when I need a pick-me-up? Sorry to say, I have a shot or two of something hot and spicy. But I have no intention of asking her to switch the arrangement because I do a better job at parenting than my wife. I'm a natural nurturer. She's a hunter and corporate predator. So we go on."

As I would advise other couples in traditional arrangements, a shift in balance is needed. Something that will brighten up the stay-at-home parent's existence. Ron and his wife are currently taking steps in that direction. The moral of the story: if you're wise and have your heart and brain in the right place, fine-tune an arrangement that works rather than try fitting into one that has no chance at all.

Make sure that your values are child-friendly and partner-friendly. Never forget that just because it can be done, you must not allow yourself to be made invisible or trivial. Make sure that your wife, child, and you are in a true partnership where success is defined less by the car in your suburban driveway or a Manhattan penthouse, but by the health, happiness, and safety of the environment you've created for all of you. Don't wait for an illness or death to dictate what kind of dad you want to be.

CHAPTER 20

FATHERING IS A WORD, NOT A SENTENCE

Childhood is a symbol of all that's good, all that's pure, innocent, creative, and full of hope. It's also the metaphor for all beginnings.

You might innocently believe that your decision to have a child was in order for you to have a child. Think again. Think of it in broader terms. Barring accidents (were they truly?), you and your partner have purposefully and mindfully chosen to give the gift of life to a child, and a gift of the child to the world. You held the divine cup, sipped of the nectar that animates us all, and breathed life into a new being—who from that moment on is entrusted to you. Your mission, which you have chosen to accept, is helping to shape this wondrous bundle of potential into its best possible actualization. The better you become at accomplishing this task, the happier the child's life will be, long into adulthood, and the better the world will be for generations to come. Awesome, but you can do it!

Once you have embraced this shift in your role, your relationship with the child becomes totally different from perceiving him as your property. The child is an individual. There has never been, nor will there ever be, another exactly like him. He does not belong to you. He belongs to himself and to the world, and your responsibility is that of a loving and wise custodian.

You must do whatever it takes to keep yourself in good condition. Ask yourself daily what you must do to get to and then remain in top form. You don't want your child to become a chore or a burden. Insist on what you need. Don't ever feel sorry for yourself when the going gets rough. The cliché that the love you give is the love you get may or may not prove true. The key word in this is *give*. Receiving is the icing on the cake and it is something that cannot be demanded. The more competent you become at fathering, the more you will receive from your child. And giving entails more than the child. When you give to the mother of your child, it's not only generosity; it's the best way to take care of yourself.

A child is not a pet. There's no kennel that will take him back. Fathering is for life—yours and his. The child will carry your image for as long as he lives. You will be his point of reference long after you're no more. A little voice will keep reminding him: "What would Dad have done in this situation? How would he feel about it?"

Have the wisdom to know how deeply to become involved and when to step back and how far. A benevolent father will take his child to the playground, show him the ropes, and then step back to allow the child to risk venturing out, yet stay close enough to prevent him from getting hurt. If you try to shield him completely, he will never learn how to recover from pain.

Enjoy your child. Have a ball!

Fathering is the greatest trip there is.

PART II

FATHER AND HIS CHILD

Chapter 21

Boy? Girl? (So Long as It's a Boy)

Fathering is a musical instrument that resides inside each of us, only to be discovered the moment our child is born. The easiest melodies to master are the ones we've heard our parents play. If we are unconscious parents, we become virtuosos in only those tunes, and every time the occasion arises we pick up our instrument and blast away. But the sweetest melodies take lots of practice and may sound dissonant at first. Taking our time, practicing diligently and lovingly and with a conscious and generous mind, the instrument begins to sing like a Stradivarius, filling us with compositions worthy of the greatest artists.

"Most men prefer boys, but I'm hoping for a girl," said Gordon shyly, perhaps with a hint of embarrassment. Like many of my clients, Gordon looks back to a troubled childhood. (A cynical friend of mine stoutly maintains that if you had a fantastic childhood, you have a bad memory.) Gordon's memory is very clear if somewhat skewed. What he remembers mostly about his mother was her comment, oft repeated: "You and I both know we would all have been better served if you were never born."

"So why do you want a girl?" I asked.

"A girl is more likely to be raised by my wife, who comes from a solid home. You know how you always say that if you're left to your own devices you'll repeat your parents' mistakes. I would be more likely to do that with a son. I would kill myself if I ever produced another me."

I had a whole barrage of arguments ready to fire: that he was a great guy (despite his unwholesome opinion of himself) and that I had been referring to unconscious parents, not clear-thinking, sensitive, thoughtful, receptive, and considerate men like him—but I decided to defer these comments to another time. I knew we would just spiral down into a theoretical discussion.

"Other than turning out like you, can you think of any other reasons?"

"I'm not very good at sports. Would you believe I've never been to a hockey game? To tell you the truth, I've never felt very manly. I remember my father being flabbergasted that I couldn't do a chin-up when I was twelve. He made a big show of it at my aunt's picnic. My aunt had a picnic every August and there was this swing set in the backyard. I was the only one out of five or six boys who couldn't do a chin-up."

"So what did you do then?"

"I snuck off to the house and cried in the bathroom."

"And then what did you do?"

"I started lifting weights, after school."

"And a year later, as I remember, you could do fifty chin-ups. Does that tell you anything?"

"Yeah. I hated my father."

I could identify with Gordon on several levels. I too had a great deal of difficulty with my father for many years. With age and therapy, not to mention having experienced fatherhood myself, I've become much more inclined to forgiveness.

Since I was raised in Hungary, I've never developed a serious taste for hockey, football, wrestling, demolition derby, and other macho pastimes. I prefer listening to great jazz on the sound system of my car to the exhaust of my neighbor's Harley. To retain the wonder and fascination of plumbing, gas, and electricity in our home, I've resolved not to delve into their mysteries and demystify them into mere utilities.

My wife considers me a handyman par excellence when I change a fuse and the lights come back on. I hate camping and army surplus outlets. Hardware stores bore me to death. An American urban male I'm not.

When my third child was born a son, I was scared for him, and for me, for about thirty seconds. Then, a wave of intense joy and loving swept away all self-doubt and apocalyptic thought. And I'm pleased to say that this wave has only gathered momentum over the past twenty-two years. I comforted myself with the notion that not being macho was not so bad. My boy would learn how to turn a basket of raw ingredients into a sumptuous and cholesterol-wise Mediterranean meal. He'd get first-rate training in dancing a mean salsa and a lifelong education on why no idea is worth risking a life for, qualities that are not likely to get him on the football team but will probably add to his lifelong enjoyment of being alive.

As much as I love all my children equally, with my son I developed a parallel relationship of camaraderie. Just as women talk differently among themselves, so do men. My heart burst with pride when his third-grade teacher informed me that my son was known for two things: making peace with adversaries, and being popular with the girls because he knew "how to talk to women," quoting one of his classmates of the same age. His popcorn-golden curls helped, added the teacher.

Around that time, however, we also discovered that we each had a dark side, me not for the first time. After my son had pushed his three-year-old sister down the stairs, and his explanation was that he "felt like it," I slapped him in the face. This was so out of character for me that whenever I think of it I still feel an ache. It was a blow that shattered my son's innocent and complete trust in his father as a powerful, benevolent soul mate. He learned that power can cut both ways: it can hurt as well as protect.

Why did I do it and what have I learned from it? This question preoccupied me for years. After I laboriously taught my son about the evils of violence, how could I have betrayed it all in such a blatant fashion? Although most parents might dismiss the slap as well justified, nonviolence was at the core of what I believed a good parent should be—and still do.

To try to forgive myself, I resorted to the recognition that I was not perfect, or rather that I was just a human being, who like everybody else can be driven to such anger that the hand follows.

To this day, neither one of us knows why he pushed his little sister down the stairs. What I do know is that it was a useless and *harmful* question to ask him why he did it. We never really know why we do things. It just happened, without rationally deciding to do so. He was there, she was there, he had nothing else to do. So, he just did it. It's that simple. And the same thing is pretty much true for me: I don't believe in hitting, I reacted without thinking. Not a good idea at all. This, however, doesn't mean that either one of us was not responsible for what we did. As such, there must be consequences. But hitting is not an acceptable consequence.

There was fear about my son's lack of empathy.

My own punishment was swift. My son told the neighborhood, my friends, my associates, and indeed anyone who came into the house and was willing to listen that "my father slapped me in the face." Finally, years later, I sat him down. "Don't you think it's time we put this to rest?" He nodded and that was the end of it.

Like every human being on earth, children need to be loved. We need to show our children how lovable they are. And as fathers perhaps we need to practice this melody more deliberately with our boys than with our daughters. It just seems to play much more spontaneously with girls. We live in a homophobic culture. With sons, many fathers worry excessively about sissifying the little tyke and therefore withhold open demonstrations of affection.

We owe our children of both genders a secure grounding in love. If we don't show them our love they lose the capacity to love themselves. Just as important is the love they see between their parents. They need to see their fathers' being loving, caring, and responsible toward their mothers since this will be the foundation for their future pairing and parenting. Lastly, we must also treat ourselves with mindful kindness—being conscious of what we want and do not want—and never skulk away into martyrdom.

Gordon thought that his wife would be a better role model for a girl than he would be for a boy. What he failed to appreciate was that putting the welfare of his unborn child ahead of his own was an instance of paternal generosity. He was already planting the seed of self-worth in his unborn child, thus putting himself far ahead of the pack.

Gordon's prayer for a girl was answered. Later, I heard they had a son, and then twin boys. Although I have not seen Gordon since his daughter was born, I am convinced the boys turned out just fine, with Gordon as a perfectly competent father.

CHAPTER 22

DON'T PUT YOUR BABY TO WORK

An armchair philosopher (it might've been me) once said that the proof of the existence of altruism is one's conscious choice to become a parent. Not only does parenting appear to present lots of opportunities for selflessness, it also demands it. I could also argue, however, that the altruism of parenting is an illusion. Apparently selfless acts towards our children are often immediately repaid, or else become a secured mortgage on which we collect for life.

We all have private wishes, dreams, goals, and aspirations for our kids. Or maybe we just want them to be happy. So be it. But to the extent that secret and often unconscious motives play a part, we have to become aware of the pervasive effect they have on our daily interactions with our children.

To unearth those furtive thoughts takes work, honesty, and a painful baring of the soul. To look them squarely in the eye, no matter how outlandish, embarrassing, or fiendish they may be, takes a lot of courage. But we're not done yet. What we must do then, after all that painstaking exploration, is to take the knowledge we have gleaned and store it in an unlit corner of our minds. Yes, we can pull it out and thumb through the contents in private, just to keep us from going astray, but we must never and I mean never share that knowledge with our kids. Our secret desires are *our* desires and not our children's.

How often have you heard somebody say: "I want to give my child everything I never had." It's hard not to yield to the temptation of righting past wrongs through our children. But our children come into this world innocent of the injustices we've suffered decades ago. If we try to make up for our childhood pain by preventing them from having similar experiences, we will end up making them defenseless precisely against those experiences from which we tried to protect them.

You may want your kid to be the youngest Nobel Prize winner, a Michael Jordan, or Bill Gates' financial advisor, or a Jerry

Seinfeld. Keep it all to yourself!

I read in the newspaper several years ago the account of a teen-aged boy in California, who was forced by his trainer to dive from a ten-meter board before he was up to the task, and when he tried, he broke his neck and ended up paralyzed. That alone would have been tragic but it turned out that the trainer was also the boy's father, a competition diver who once placed fourth in the Olympics.

It is often difficult to separate oneself from one's children and remember that we are not the same, that our goals are our own business. Because we bring our children up from the time they are totally dependent and because they are so eager to learn and imitate everything we do, it is easy to fall into the trap of considering them extensions of ourselves. The tragic tale of the child with the broken neck is just an extreme example of what you and I are prone to do on a daily basis if we don't stop and really think.

When my children were still quite young, I had a fantasy about building the Stein Medical Center, staffed by my kids and myself. Each of my children would be a doctor in some life and death specialty, while I would be sitting in the hub as the resident psychotherapist. Unfortunately, because the idea was so compelling, I failed to keep it to myself. We kidded about it now and then, without anyone in the household objecting. When my fourth child was born, I had an actual dream in which she grew up to become a rabbi. As I mulled it over, instead of inhabiting my medical center fantasy I saw her as an overseer, a supreme being.

It took some time before I could understand the building blocks of my fantasy. I was positioning my children in a circle around me to guard me from illness and death. Three would take care of keeping me in excellent health and prolonging my life, while the fourth would minister to my needs as I passed through the Pearly Gates.

Little did I know that at least one of my children was deeply troubled by my "innocent" fantasy, carrying it for years without letting on. When the time came for choosing a career, Cybèle came to me in tears: "Daddy, I don't want to be a doctor."

I have to tell you that this is a serious matter. The unaware father (or mother) will tend to play out his hidden desires on his child. Get help if you need to, or do whatever it takes to get a handle on those devils. A child is not a canvas.

The moral: beware of motives, particularly when they seem altruistic.

CHAPTER 23

BABIES ARE BORING

If you think babies are boring, you haven't really paid attention. Men sometimes have high expectations of their children, so that when they are still babies, they check them each day for unusual achievements and signs of superhuman intelligence. Of course, the babies, being unaware of this, just go about their goo and gaa business as usual, while the father-inspector turns away disappointed. This is one of those instances where the unaware parent can do damage to himself, the baby, and the relationship between them. It is but a short step to one day reprimanding the child proudly coming home from school with a "B+" instead of an "A."

I have always loved the company of young children and babies, especially when they were mine, and especially around the time when some fathers are apt to complain that all the baby does is eat, shit, and sleep.

Many new dads are content seeing a nice, sweet-smelling, clean, and smiling baby. They are reassured if all fingers and toes are accounted for and if in some remote way they see some resemblance to themselves. Women often complain that we are bored with our very young kids until they can actually entertain and play with us.

Well, we know how our mind works. It's always busy plotting and strategizing, and then there are all the magazines and newspapers that have been piling up. We don't sleep so well either, what with the new baby waking us up every few hours. Let's wait until we can really communicate with the child. Right now they don't even know whether we're there or not. I'll save my strength, we might say, until I can really do some good.

Granted, there is a bit of that in us, and often it's what I call the first instinct, the response of the unaware parent. However, by spending a few minutes examining how our instincts work and do not work to our family's advantage, we can change. Why it's worth changing is that our first instinct is dead wrong, particularly in these times when we have learned so much about the early development of babies. We know for instance that the baby's first year of life is pivotal in the development of trust, self-reliance, sense of independence, and self-worth. A baby knows his mother within days of being born. If you take the time, he will also recognize you, and your influence in the baby's life can begin right away. Postponing only makes it more difficult. And most of all, practice makes pleasurable. The more relaxed time you spend with the baby, the better you'll feel, and it's very good for both of you.

Let me tell you what I personally enjoyed about my babies. I have spent literally hundreds of hours marveling at the secret messages my babies were sending me. They're constantly in communication. Just by looking at their faces, you can see a myriad subtle changes, half-formed gestures, not always perfectly symmetrical, rapid changes in skin color, in the shape and brightness of their eyes. And their naked little bodies, hands, and feet always in motion show the enjoyment of their freedom after many months of incarceration. If you look carefully enough, you'll soon find patterns, attempts to coordinate facial expressions and movements of the limbs, and you can marvel at the selections from their rich lexicon of sounds. Babies speak novels, if you spend the time to disconnect your perceptions from your internal dialogue and worldly preoccupations.

Babies like to hear their mother's voice because it's a voice they've heard from day one inside the womb. If you speak often to your baby, your voice too, over time, will develop a soothing effect. I still recall the sweet serenity of dark nights when just being with my baby was more spiritual and more meditative than anything an Eastern guru could teach me.

If you still think babies are boring, take a moment to figure out why you think so. There's a possibility that you wear a shell of boredom and the baby does not provide enough entertainment to break through. Or maybe you're just too preoccupied to notice, let alone enjoy, the tiny little pleasure signals your baby is constantly sending you. And if it requires effort to change your perception, so be it. It's time well invested.

CHAPTER 24

INSPIRATIONAL DIAPER CHANGE

For some reason, I have been blessed with a natural affinity for changing diapers and must disavow any feelings of disgust or revulsion that might be inferred from what follows. But other men tell a different story.

To watch a mother change a baby's diaper is to witness an intricately choreographed ballet for two hands. Effortlessly, in a puff of talcum, an off-smelling little bundle becomes transformed into the sweet, aromatic, cooing baby you know and love. As she hands him to you to hold, it's almost as if she were taking a bow.

We don't need to aspire to such virtuosity. The challenge we overcome is a much weightier one. It is best expressed by comments such as this: "I can't, honey. You want me to barf all over the place?" What's surprising is that she buys it. How easily she gives in to these arguments! You want to know what I think? She doesn't believe you for a minute. She lets you off the hook because she likes changing the baby.

Let me quote two pseudo-statistics:

1. Seventy-eight percent of surgeons, upon entering medical school, declare they can't stand the sight of blood. Later, making $300,000 a year, they have no qualms about handling any type of bodily fluids.

2. One of ten diaper changes in expert hands is accompanied by finger contamination. With liquid stool, the incidence increases to one in three. You have to watch very carefully to catch mother in the act. You see, she doesn't scream out loud: "My god, I got some on my finger! Come, help." She merely goes on with the job and at the end surreptitiously cleans her finger with an unused corner of the wet-wipe.

So how do we overcome this innate, organic, masculine resistance to the smell and sight of, how should I put it, shit, and the horror of getting the stuff on our hands? I can only tell you how one of my clients did it.

1. "I decided it was important. A rational decision to act in a certain way in advance makes it much easier for us men to follow through. We are good at that: organized thinking, discipline, and sacrifice and carrying out a plan. After all, lives can depend on us.

2. "I reasoned that since I was a grown man, with grown duties and responsibilities, I wasn't going to let a little thing like baby shit get in the way of doing what I thought was important for my self-esteem and for my partner's opinion of me.

3. "I knew I loved my baby. I just tried to think of *it* as part of her.

4. "I learned by observing my wife closely. Very closely. Sometimes this involved breathing through the mouth so as to bypass sensory fibers in my nostrils.

5. "If I had to do it today, I'd certainly use disposable diapers. Wherever you stand on the environmental issue, a few disposable diapers while you're learning will not make a lot of difference to the planet. Since there were no disposables in my day, I had to learn the harder way.

6. "I didn't wait to be asked. One Sunday morning I made sure to sneak out of bed as soon as I heard the baby stirring, snuck into her room and did it, after having rehearsed for several hours in my mind while my wife was fast asleep. Unlike most things one rehearses, this one worked out exactly as planned. You should have seen the incredulous reception when I walked into the bedroom with the baby all spruced up and a ribbon in her hair. And I'll never forget the smile on my wife's face that she just couldn't wipe off for the rest of the day."

So what he's saying is that you begin by steeling your mind. You must be intellectually determined. Once you do that, it gets easier with use. Eventually, you'll be fighting to get there first—and in the end, everybody wins.

I would be remiss if I didn't impart a few nuggets of practical wisdom. Before you actually proceed to change a diaper, make sure you have the following within easy reach:

- Two new diapers (in case of mechanical failure or defective technique).

- Plenty of wet-wipes. Take out a couple from the container before you start until you become proficient in extracting a sheet with one hand.

- Baby powder, depending on skin condition (usually optional but not always—details on this subject are covered in manuals).

- A pacifier, a rattle, or a bottle to occupy the baby while you're at work.

- A washable changing surface is recommended for beginners. You'll notice mom using a sparkling white sheet under the baby. Don't pay any attention; she's only showing off. You can pre-warm a plastic mat by running warm water over it.

- A moist rag or towel that can clean up all evidence of the deed.

- A bag to take everything away.

- Oh, yes. And if it's a boy, be ready to duck.

Once you've become an expert, an optional refinement is not screwing up your face while wiping baby's bottom. You don't wish to convey to the baby, not to mention to your partner, that there's anything dirty or unpalatable about her or anything that she produces.

And one more thing. Don't rush into the act of diaper change at the first sight of a red face or the first inkling of telltale aroma around the room. Wait about five minutes. It can be disheartening to change a diaper only to find it instantly replenished.

An ecological note about diapers. Disposable diapers pollute the environment when you discard them. But reusable diapers have to be washed. Hot water uses up energy, as does a washing machine. Colgate and Palmolive use up lots of energy manufacturing liquid and solid detergents. Some of these take years to degrade. Which is better for the environment? I have no figures—but my inkling is that it's close enough to a draw that we don't need to spend much energy feeling guilty.

CHAPTER 25

THE CHILD IS NOT FATHER TO THE MAN

"If it weren't for you fucking kids, I'd have a good life." This is Keith, quoting his mom's weekly litany, religiously served up every Saturday with family breakfast.

"That was just the centerpiece," continued Keith, "you should have seen the meal!"

Keith has been a member of our Wednesday night men's group for several months now. Yet his mom's message had had such a noxious effect on him that he seemed short of breath whenever he talked about her. We'd heard the story before. "'Your father, that son of a bitch, buggered off when you guys weren't even in school yet. I had a brilliant career! Your father and you fucking kids put an end to it.' Not surprisingly, I keep telling my wife I'm not keen on the prospect of parenting and kids. She still thinks she can change me."

I get angry every time I hear a client of any age recount childhood parental torments. No child should have to suffer the insult that his very existence is offensive to his parents. I have tons of compassion for Keith's mother, abandoned, betrayed, overwhelmed, and bitter—so bitter that all she could think about was her own victimization. But Keith and his siblings had nothing to do with that. They are doubly victimized because not only have they lost their father but also a dependable, loving mother instead of the shell they were left with.

Keith, as he remembers the years of his greatest torment, was between five and seven years old. What he had in common with his brothers, both toddlers, was resourcelessness. Perhaps their mother didn't really mean every word she said. Perhaps there were other occasions where she demonstrated love and caring. But the fact of the matter is that she accused them repeatedly of being responsible for her unhappiness, thus making sure the message was driven home. The mere uttering of the words was an aggressive act, not likely to ever be forgotten—or forgiven.

A memory: I'm eight years old. The war against Jews was ostensibly over, at least to the extent that the shooting and looting had ceased. But the ravage of horrors was still stretching across our mental landscape like the barbed wire all around us, as if it had grown roots deep inside our bodies. I already knew with a cursed sense of clarity that I would never see my mom again. Whatever can that mean to a child that young—the end of the world? But I kept obstinately silent, though it was ever present in my mind, probably to avoid rocking my father's unstable existence. After all, he had almost certainly lost his wife and he wasn't quite the picture of stability to begin with. Every time he came to the edge of his ability tether, he'd explode, "I should have died, not your mother. You have no use for me. I'm good for nothing. I can't take care of me, let alone you. I should just disappear; it would be much better for you." There it goes again: having lost a parent, the threat of being abandoned by the second. How can you not think unworthy thoughts of yourself when your remaining parent voices a desire to abandon you and leave you to fend for yourself?

As much as I tried, I really didn't have the emotional means to take care of both of us. So I lied. I reassured him that he was an excellent father and mother all rolled into one, and that I would help him take care of us both. The rest of the time I was silent and invisible. He never knew when I hurt, was hungry, or had a nightmare.

"My wife doesn't want to hear my childhood stories anymore," said Keith to the group, sounding hurt and resentful. "She used to keep after me all the time about not expressing my feelings. That I kept everything bottled up. And then, one day I burst, scattering debris like hot ashes after a volcanic eruption. It's true. Ever since I can remember, I was told to keep my troubles to myself. My mother would say, 'We all have our crosses to bear,' if I ever dared to complain about some pain or ache. 'You don't see me blabbering all over the place.'"

Keith's story and the stories of millions of children who feel threatened in the very essence of their survival call out in unison: don't burden your young child with your victimization, whatever it may be. If the memory of your own childhood includes dark chapters—and whose doesn't?—do not share them with your young child. It's not his fault and he cannot help you. Your child is a blank slate. Do you want to clutter those early, life-forming moments with mournful toils and troubles that don't belong to him, instead of sunshine and optimism and plenty of open space?

All the feelings, thoughts, recollections of you the parent that rise to the surface of your awareness, whether good or bad, must be honored. Just as it is vital to the child, your own thoughts need to be heard, validated, and empathized with. But wherever you chose to unburden yourself, it should not be on top of your child, who can only be smothered by it. The truth is that more than ever before, you need safe adults in a safe place, with whom you can acknowledge and heal the wounds of the past.

Hopefully, you have adults in your life: partner, friends, siblings, other relatives, a therapist, mentor, clergyman, or a men's group. For fathers, I can't stress enough the value of being in a group of men. The issue of competing with the other gender, putting the best foot forward, does not arise without women around. Look for a men's group, or start one. Don't worry about the smirking, uninformed comments by envious men and women who'll allude to men's groups as adolescents dancing in the woods, beating drums, and smelling each other's armpits.

They're only hiding their own armpits behind asinine comments. The truth is that, more than ever before, you need safe adults in a safe place with whom you can acknowledge and heal the wounds of the past so that you don't go on bleeding all over your child. You both deserve to be free of pain.

CHAPTER 26

CHILDREN ARE BUILT TO LAST

A week after she was born, we brought my firstborn, Cybèle, home from the hospital. For the first time, we were totally alone with her—and scared out of our wits. Neither my wife nor I had a clue about what to do with a newborn. The long ride across the Bay to our home in Berkeley lulled her into a deep sleep, oblivious to her parents' teetering on the edge of panic.

As recently as forty years ago, there were no courses on childbirth and no books of any value on early parent education. Not that this was a big deal for all expectant fathers, since for some the care of newborns was not in their job description.

"How will this baby survive us?" I asked rhetorically. This was unwise since my wife had been relying on my strength. I looked over, hoping for reassurance, but saw her instead trying to hide her tears in Kleenex. The implication that we might actually do her irreparable harm should never have left my lips. Our ignorance, our ineptitude, our blundering could kill her. This little creature the length of my forearm seemed so delicate, so vulnerable. Just holding her badly could snap her spine. How could we possibly succeed in keeping her alive? This may have seemed like truth to me at the time, but sharing it with my wife was an instance where complete honesty proved to be the worst policy. Soon we were both bawling like children lost in the woods, with dark setting in.

Since my teens, I had longed for a family of my own, probably because most of my family of origin had disappeared into the Nazi night. More than anything else, I wanted a child to love and care for in an atmosphere of freedom, peace, and security. The abandonment I had experienced when I was eight, when my parents were taken away, remained a deep and ever-present chasm in the pit of my stomach.

Therefore, not being hands-on, in every phase of my baby's life, was not even a remote consideration. Because of this (and quite a few other things), I was considered an oddball, even in the hip Berkeley and San Francisco communities.

It was that passionate commitment to the bond with my child that fuelled my determination to be present at Cybèle's birth. In spite of hospital policy, my wish to witness my child's birth prevailed. Cybèle was the first baby born at the University of California Medical Center with a father in the delivery room.

When we took our baby home, we needed help, definitely. There was no family around. But luckily there were Helen and Sandy! Helen and Sandy, our wonderfully warm and generous friends, had adopted a baby girl the year before. We'd spoken daily before Cybèle's arrival.

Everything Helen and Sandy had learned in the past year they proceeded to teach us, gently and patiently. We practically camped at their home, then came for just brief daily visits. After a month of wading in the shallows, we found our sea legs. Not that we'd become entirely carefree, but the occasional phone support was all we needed to have the confidence to carry on.

Apart from granting us instant relief from terror, they also bestowed on us a second gift, which as it turned out lasted through many years and many children: the name and phone number of their pediatrician.

Dr. C. (perhaps for Santa Claus?), an immensely wise and human physician, guided us expertly, with huge doses of common sense. His parenting wisdom, which he shared generously, was not something we could have otherwise found on our own.

"Relax," he said to us on our first visit. "You will not harm your daughter because you love her and because you are responsible and smart people. And even if you screw up now and then, children are built to last. You won't do anything irreparable that will mark her for life."

"What if I drop her?" I asked.

"Well, you pick her up! But you won't drop her, André. I'm sure at some point in your life you played a passable game of football. Hold her like a ball, firmly in the crook of your arm, close to your body so that you can both feel each other's warmth. You're not in the habit of dropping things you don't care about; why would you be dropping your baby? Not very likely."

And so it was decided. Dropping the baby was not an option.

"But how do I know what she needs? How do I know if she has cramps, needs food or water, or if the diaper is burning her bottom?" That I felt profoundly incompetent is an understatement.

I was a graduate student at one of the world's prestigious universities, and I had no clue about how to read my baby.

"Every baby comes with a built-in dictionary," he said, "only it's in a foreign language, and not language only. It's part charade, part voice. If you spend enough time with the child, and I don't mean reading the paper, but watching and listening, the language will come to you. Every baby has a different language, but parents who pay attention master it very quickly and effortlessly."

"The biggest challenge for you as new parents," he said on another occasion, "is your responsibility to take care of each other and yourselves. Without that, you'll be of no use to Cybèle. Take turns at night so that one of you actually sleeps. You are not to become house prisoners. Visit friends, go to concerts, and eat Chinese food. Take her with you. If you start feeling that Cybèle is a sacrifice, you'll start resenting the time you spend looking after her. That can start a chain—a chain you must avoid."

There was another problem that had been nagging me for weeks, one that I hadn't actually formulated in my mind, but when Dr. C. started speaking about it, I realized why I had been secretly brooding. "André, some fathers feel they are not as swift with the baby as mom is. There is no great mystery in that. Mom has a head start, nine months to be exact. She knows from the word go that there is intelligent life inside, and the two communicate. We men on the other hand need to be convinced."

"Whew. You mean that's it?" I asked.

"It's how it begins. But you don't have to stay there. You may be starting with a handicap but you can be as good as you want to become."

I have never forgotten his words. As I grew older and more experienced, I have added insights of my own. For instance, there is an old self-putdown, passed down through generations, that men are not nurturers. I can tell you from my personal and clinical experience that this is simply a lie. Granted, men are not always first out of the gate, but their ability to nurture is limited only by their will and commitment.

In a balanced household, each parent contributes a slightly different version of parent's milk. Of course they overlap, but they're both delicious and extremely nutritious, particularly if taken in the right proportions.

Traditionally, mother's milk is easier to digest. It is sweet and soothing, providing an immediate sense of belonging, security, grounding, and self-confidence. Father's milk is a bit lumpier but more concentrated, and may be hard to digest at first. Father's milk is also more varied, leading to a love for adventure and daring and exploration and healthy ambition. Mother's milk makes you happy to be at home. Father's milk gives you the courage to leave and to roam.

The kicker is that not many homes have a traditional balance. Sometimes the roles are completely reversed, but more often there is a mix of traditional and nontraditional influences. Sometimes one parent has a lot of milk while the other is on the thin side. The family balance cannot be prejudged by observation and an appropriate balance cannot be prescribed. The baby is usually able to work it out because he doesn't come into this world with attitude. As long as he gets the complete package, why care about the mix?

CHAPTER 27

DON'T MAKE "DADDY, I HARDLY KNEW YE" YOUR CHILD'S FAVORITE TUNE

My father passed away twenty-five years ago. He was seventy-four and I was forty-two. It's strange, as it seems I've had more of a relationship with him since he became an angel than while he was on earth. How is that possible, you may ask. Because now I have him in me, and he's not here to be absent, dismissing, judgmental, and otherwise detached from me. When he was alive, I had only faint and fleeting moments when I felt that I mattered. I've been cherishing those rare memories because they're proof positive that my father loved me with the kind of love that I've been promoting throughout this book—putting your child first when you hurt the most. I'll give just one example of what I mean, perhaps the most tangible evidence that he held my well-being at a greater priority than his.

In October 1956, I escaped from life, if you can call it such, under Communism in Budapest, Hungary. My dad had a sister who had been living in Paris for decades. She welcomed me into her home, and life could start over, this time on the right foot. I felt that, finally, anything I was willing to work for was possible. In spite of my father spending most of his waking hours working and in self-imposed silent exile at the bottom of the armchair, I missed him—he was the only father I ever had. In August 1957, with help from my aunt, he could visit me in Paris for two weeks. During that visit we walked the streets of Paris, he and I, without many words. I felt his presence more than ever before. I knew he came to be with me. A street photographer took a snapshot of us on a boulevard. I still have it in a prime spot in my office. Often I look at the picture and I speak to him. He's, like God, only present by his absence and silence, but he's there anyway and it's a comfort. At other times, when no one is available to hear my inner fears and anxieties, I tell them and weep. This time, he doesn't say "Get ahold of yourself, people are watching" as he did in January 1966 at Oakland International Airport when I feared for my baby's life. This time it's just him and me. My daddy.

At the end of those two wonderful weeks in Paris, I took him to his train and we had to say goodbye. He was already standing on the steps of the train car with tears in his eyes—the first time since he found out my mom didn't come back from Nazi deportation. "I know you're an adult now and I've no business telling you what to do, but this is the last order I'll ever give you. Don't ever even think of coming back because of me. You've a future here; back there it's hell. And I'll die soon enough and you'll have come home for nothing." He could scarcely control the flow of his tears. His thick, coke-bottle bottom glasses looked like there was a storm raging behind them. I wanted to jump on the step to hug him real tight, to transfer my youthful strength and the vigor of my love to his frail body, nourishment for the trip, so to speak, and I don't mean Paris to Budapest. But he turned around and disappeared on the train. He didn't come to the window to wave goodbye. He was really gone. That void had to keep me company for nine years until we met again.

Why is he telling this sappy slop in this book, you may wonder. Isn't this a bit self-indulgent? Perhaps, just a tad. But let me tell you a secret. I'm writing this book as a gift to you young fathers, and it is also a way to reconcile with me as a young child with and without my dad.

The immediate reason for this digression is not only grounded in my story, but it is one that I've been hearing from many men and women in and out of my practice.

"For the longest time," one fellow in the men's group told us with a huge lump in his throat, "I swear I didn't know who was sitting behind that newspaper held by two sets of fingers. I *thought* it was my dad, but I couldn't be sure." I've heard many similar recollections from former children. "When I was eight," a friend of mine shared with me sometime ago, "I felt like calling my dad 'Gazette,' because where his forehead was supposed to be, I found night after night the word 'Gazette,' his daily replacement of life and me."

Other fathers are absent from their young children's family life by working too long hours, or spending their leisure moments with their buddies at the pub, the races, playing cards, and yes, with another woman (not always the same). And yet others, they're there like my dad, without really being there, prisoners of their depression. Some dads spend much of their time on the road, in planes, hotels—out of town. Some of it is work; some of it is escape. "As a kid," my friend Steve told me, "I had the distinct impression that he was escaping from me. I was not fun enough, good enough, or something not enough for him to want to be home, with me."

Beyond the self-centered outlook of children, Steve was probably right. He wasn't important enough for his dad to be home. His dad thought the father's love is demonstrated by and limited to providing for the family financially. He was deadly wrong. And I mean deadly because as I've been keeping company with all the sad young men simmering in the grief of father hunger, I realized what they—we—have lost. *Please*, please make sure this won't be *your* child's memory of you.

I know it's not always a piece of cake, but you can arrange your other activities in such a manner that you put your child first. You tell yourself, "No matter what, every day I'll spend X amount of time with my child." And then you arrange the rest of your schedule as if that blocked-off time didn't exist. Much like financial planners recommend that you pay yourself before you pay your bills. Before you agree to go on a trip, ask yourself, "Is this indispensable? What would be the consequence if I didn't go? How else could the matter at hand be addressed?" If you must go, ask yourself how long do I *really* have to be away? And how long do I want to be away from my child (and partner)? Remind yourself that this is not a favor you're doing for your child; this is the investment in her well-being, self-esteem, and concept of male-female relationships. And I do hope that it's a gift you give yourself when you hang out with your child in a mindful fashion. Yes, it can be done (I can already see some of you objecting to the concept). If your partner can rearrange her entire life around motherhood, so can you. We tend to bellyache about not feeling important enough in our children's life. The first level of exclusion is perpetrated by fathers themselves. Don't be a victim of your alienation from your child and yourself as a father.

CHAPTER 28

CHIP OFF THE OLD BLOCK

What greater joy for a kid, especially for a son, to be told that he is just like Dad? After all, for young boys, father is the A to Z of all men. Whatever he says goes. Being a chip off the old block is usually considered a compliment, except when it's not: "You're just like your father!" or "The apple doesn't fall far from the tree."

I recall when my son was a mere eighteen months old, I bought us a pair of navy blue sailor sweaters with white trim and an embroidered anchor on the sleeve, identical except in size. Although I bought similar sweaters for my daughters, those were in a different color. I guess it was not as pressing for my unconscious to turn my daughters into clones.

I would walk around the neighborhood, son in tow, marking territory, proudly proclaiming that this was my son and make no mistake about it. Friends as well as people I'd never met would comment, much to my delight, on how much my son resembled me.

Since I had already two daughters when my son was born, there were years of pent-up anxiety waiting in the wings. Once he was born and I'd recovered from the shock of just having become father to a boy, I became eager and impatient. Not only did I want to teach my son everything I knew but everything I was, all without a moment to waste. I wanted him to speak like me, think like me, be a pacifist, love jazz, and become a gourmet cook. I had his whole life planned out before me.

Having an offspring who is every bit like you, only a superior version, is a dream come true. It is like reliving your life and erasing past mistakes on the fly. Ah, but what a burden for the little guy!

A chip off the old block is in danger of remaining just that, a chip, without much hope of becoming his own block. Although I was already a psychotherapist, familiar with the pits and foibles of child-parent interactions (in my clients and other people in general) insight into what I was really doing came to me like a flying tackle out of nowhere, leading me into a prolonged period of soul-searching and re-evaluation. I wish I could say that the sudden revelation that I was cloning myself was self-generated, but the truth of it is that it was my son, who at about age three began vigorously resisting my programming efforts.

Like all wise psychotherapists, I had a therapist of my own, who gradually helped me face the choice that had to be made to relinquish those efforts of molding my son in my image. It took time to internalize what I knew to be the truth and what I have been preaching to my clients for years, that my son was an individual, that he was not me, that I did not own him, and that if I persisted in that notion I would be doing him irreparable harm.

As for my son, I could certainly not be looking for help from him. Sensing my uncertainty and realizing that by some good fortune he'd suddenly gained the upper hand, my son went totally overboard. For a long time I was unable to teach him anything at all. He wouldn't even accept help learning to ride his new tricycle. His standard response to suggestions in all fields of endeavor was "I know. I know that!"

Trying to create miniature clones of ourselves will backfire. The intention may come from a loving place, but it is also an unhealthy place. Children have their own genetic makeup and their own destiny. In passing through childhood they will pick and select those attributes they wish to adopt. We are there to provide safety and shelter and guidance, as long as it is of the non-self-serving variety. Are any of us so enamored of our own perfection?

If we do our jobs right, our children will emulate those characteristics we admire in ourselves and reject those we dislike. Unless you're a total degenerate, and perhaps even then, your child will turn out a bit or a lot like you. In some respects, in spite of my early errant ways, my son has "chosen" to be not unlike me. When he sees people in trouble, he stops to help. He has compassion for the underdog and is repulsed by prejudice. While many of his friends are prone to get down and dirty in adversity, my son uses humor to slide on to a lighter plain. He appreciates clothes and likes to borrow mine. Though his room is still (a bit) messier than my study.

I like to think that the ways in which he resembles me demonstrate a vote of confidence in who I am, though this may be dreaming. Certainly, not everything he adopted is positive. But I do hope that what is will be remembered as a gift from me to him.

Now that we have become aware of the pitfalls, we can avoid subjecting our children to much of our cloning efforts. In every chapter of this book, I try to show how gaining awareness can lead to a healthier and more temperate resolution to problems. Who doesn't want the best for their kids? With a roadmap (examining our inclinations), the maze becomes navigable, if not exactly a walk in the park. And one more thing! When you want the best for your child, remember well that good enough has to be good enough.

My son Adrian when he was sixteen said to me, at the conclusion of a father-son discussion, "Dad, don't take this the wrong way, but my job now is to find fault with everything about you. And I reserve the right to change my conclusions at a later date." He did. And he didn't. We can both live with and coexist with our own truths.

CHAPTER 29

FOOD FOR THOUGHT

"Michael has always been a finicky eater but what happened last week felt like he hit me on the head with a hammer," said Margaret, a client of mine some years ago, talking about her ten-year-old. "I was rather down last week as you know, so I wasn't being a great mom and feeling guilty about that, so I figured I'd make up for it by cooking him a feast with all the things he seemed to like recently, since his tastes seem to change monthly. I made this fabulous dinner for the two of us: roast beef, mashed potatoes, asparagus, Caesar salad, and a great chocolate fudge cake. I put it out all at once to show him the feast. What do you think his reaction was? He ran to the bathroom and barfed or maybe just pretended, I don't know. What a kick in the teeth! He must hate me. There's no other explanation. All that work for nothing and these things aren't cheap either."

This is an extreme version of the food drama enacted in millions of homes from the time the child is old enough to be fed. In this particular case there was no father in the house, but in my experience fathers tend to wash their hands concerning matters of food, as if they considered this a private affair between mom and child, with the occasional exception of the autocratic father who'll say, "You eat what's on the table or you go to bed hungry."

In my version of good-enough fathering, we take an active role in what goes into our children's mouths, just as we participate in every other aspect of our children's lives. We can lament till doomsday about how our partners keep us alienated from our children, or how our culture has straightjacketed us into the role of the banker. Yet, if we are not willing to get our hands dirty, dealing with everything concerning our children, whether it is pleasant or difficult, our complaining falls through the sieve of reason.

I am a huge fan of free will. That means I choose what I want to do and what I am not willing to do and live with the consequences of my choice. To wit, in the opening act of the human drama, God gave Adam and Eve freedom to do anything, but they were not allowed to eat the apple from the forbidden tree. He didn't take away their free will but put them on notice that if they broke his commandment there would be consequences. I suggest to you that you do your best to live by your free will and avoid putting yourself into situations where the outcome is just not acceptable, no matter what.

If you aspire to being a truly nurturing dad, involve yourself with your child's nutrition. It helps if you discuss it with your partner to see if you can agree on how to deal with your child's eating habits before problems arise, which may be as early as three months. Opinions will range from those of the autocratic dad quoted earlier to the opposite extreme, where a parent will search the universe for a morsel the child will accept into his mouth and actually swallow. Coming to a mutual agreement from polar opposites may be a Herculean task, yet compared to the perpetual squabbling at every meal for twenty years it is but a soak in the tub. Between these extremes are countless variations and I don't propose to tell you the right way because attitudes about putting food into one's mouth are so fundamentally ingrained into our psyche that there is not one right way that every parent can accept.

Yet, because the topic is hugely controversial, I feel I must take a stance, if for no other reason than to prevent you from trying to adopt some self-styled expert's dogmatic approach.

Men and women in our urban culture have different concepts about, and relationship with, food and eating. We men have not been targeted to the same extent by the media and other image molders to fit size 2 or smaller. As a result, there is greater tolerance for boys indulging in junk foods than girls. A balancing factor is that boys engage in more fat-burning activities than girls. Girls are cynically squeezed between two waves of advertising: to be thin, beautiful, and desirable, and to eat junk food. To make matters more intolerable, let's take away from them opportunities of competitive sports in the school curriculum, such as swimming, track and field, soccer, and hockey, to name a few.

Mothers, usually in charge of shopping, school lunches, and snacks, tend to have a bigger say in a child's nutrition. Since large numbers of women have also fallen into the beauty trap, their approach to their children's nutrition is necessarily tainted by their own eating drama. As if this were not enough, Mom feels unappreciated and unloved if the child refuses the food she puts in front of her child, interpreting this as a personal rejection.

Mother needs our help. We need to express our own appreciation when we sit down at every meal, letting her feel that the drudgery of daily meal preparation is worthwhile, while also setting an example to our children. We also need to comment on how much we enjoy her creations. If she is a lousy cook, and some are, take a cooking course together or do the cooking yourself. Eating together is more important in family dynamics than anyone would suspect.

There are many families that don't sit down to eat, except maybe once a week if they're lucky. Coming from a European background, I find this personally astounding. Professionally, I think it is playing with fire, tantamount to setting a fuse to the nucleus of the nuclear family. I am fully taking into account that parents may work shifts, that there are night classes, meetings, and a host of other obligations parents have to fulfill. I can only urge you to juggle your schedule in such a way that you can all sit down to a meal at least three times a week and once on the weekend, starting when the child is but a few months old. And it can't be a stressed affair. If the dinner table turns into a battlefield, nobody is going to get any nourishment. If possible, allow at least half an hour before and after the meal before you rush off. If you find this impossible to carry out, at least one parent should be present at these meals; otherwise, you may find that maintaining a cohesive family unit becomes an unreachable dream.

Men who do not to take a shared responsibility are passively condoning the status quo. By not showing healthy eating by example, fathers must assume equal part of the blame. Learn about nutrition—what makes for a balanced diet and what prepared foods to avoid.

In order to feed proper and delicious meals to my children, I learned to cook. (No, my wife is not a lousy cook, and if she were, would I dare say it?) This way I know what they eat and how much. It is not only a health benefit but it is a very intimate and hands-on way to be nourishing. From the time they have started to eat solid food, I have taken a real pleasure in not only serving them good food but also food that looked good and fun, arranging it on the plate or serving dish in a manner pleasing to the eye. Finally, cooking a varied diet introduces children to new tastes that open up possibilities for a wide variety of ethnic cuisines. Not only are they often healthier than our North American diet, but the child will be able to sit down with neighbors without gagging.

All too often, finishing what is on the child's plate is a concern. Make a joint decision on how to deal with this. If I can make an obvious suggestion, start with doling out a small portion. One of the nightmares of my childhood was the coercion to eat everything on my plate, whether I was hungry or not, whether I found what was put in front of me palatable or disgusting. My earliest memories of table politics centered around the unchallengeable rule of my father's (and I believe my mother's, but I have too little memory of her to be sure): "You must eat what is on your plate, no exception. If you don't eat it for dinner, you'll have it for breakfast. Or for lunch, or the next dinner. Nothing gets thrown out."

I'll never forget a particular meal when I was around six. I was served something that looked like cream of spinach, which I loved (not bad for a little kid!), but it sure didn't smell or taste like spinach. My father insisted that it was spinach. And as usual, I had to eat it to the last spoonful. If he had put camel shit in front of me, I wouldn't have found it more repulsive. I had tears in my eyes as I stared at my plate that just didn't want to disappear no matter how hard I prayed God to make it go away. When I looked at my father pleadingly for mercy, I noticed that he had a plate of sweet peas in front of him. I asked him, not in so many words, where the democracy went in this household. He got angry: "Don't question your father. You eat what you're given. Besides, you need the vitamins, I don't." That was that. Later I found out the damn thing was Swiss chard.

Perhaps as a result, I never coaxed my children too strongly to eat anything they had an aversion for. As they became older, I included them in the menu planning before shopping, whenever possible. None of them ever had to eat more than they wanted. You wouldn't hear too much of "This bite is for mommy, this one's for daddy . . . this one's for great-uncle Willy on your mother's side." I never blackmailed them with "I took all this trouble cooking it, the least you can do is eat it." Although it seems to roll off the tongue oh so naturally, I would also refrain from "Shame on you. There're millions of African children starving to death."

We're so fortunate on this continent to have a wide variety of food to pick from that we may as well buy stuff that we know they will eat without torment. At the same time, I like to introduce new foods as tasters, gastronomic curiosities, available for them to try should they wish to. There's always a chance that these could become staples, although admittedly I have only met with mixed success.

What about junk food? While universally vilified, not all junk food is junk. A properly prepared lean hamburger is not junk food, especially if accompanied by veggies instead of fries. Nor do I deprive my kids of the occasional junk candy treats, Cheezies, chips, or other "foodoids" that they tend to ram down with such delight. My favorite was declaring Fridays junk treat days. They were allowed to pick their poison for lunch to their eyes' content.

To this day, our children are poor consumers for the junk food merchants, yet without feeling deprived. Now and then I buy some really good, righteous chocolate, so intensely chocolate that a little piece goes a long way, and then share it in the family way.

CHAPTER 30

THE TRUTH WILL SET YOU FREE

"As you know, I've had a really rough and rocky childhood," Gabe, an old friend from Budapest, told me over a cup of tea at Dooney's, my local café, hideaway, office (that is where I'm writing these words). Gabe and I go way back to second grade. Life decisions and their consequences turned us in opposite directions. After having lost contact with him, I felt the need to try to find him. Thanks to the marvels of the Internet, I found him in a God-awful and people-forsaken town in Death Valley. Three months later he came to visit me in Toronto. The conversation to which I'm referring took place a few months ago.

"The worst blow of them all was when I discovered that my father had the habit of lying to everyone, including me."

"So did mine," I interjected, feeling a flip at the pit of my stomach. I knew this was not going to be an easy saunter down memory lane. "And to tell the truth, I've lied to my kids, too."

"That's a damned shame, my friend," he reflected in a somber but not judgmental tone. "I bet you've done your best teaching your kids the virtue of telling the truth. Yet, you didn't deliver on your own moral standards. What do you think that communicates to them? I was four when I realized that my father told me a colossal lie. One day my dog disappeared. I was devastated and inconsolable. My dad, not the world's most patient man, decided to take a short cut. 'Listen, my boy, Blackie will be back tomorrow or the day after. I know he got lost. You know he likes to go around sniffing. Well, he must have followed a scent too intensely and lost track of where he was going. He's got his tag. People will return him. I already talked to neighbors near and far to keep an eye out for your doggie.'

"I needed to believe him desperately, so I calmed down more or less. You didn't have a dog as a kid; you don't know what that dog meant to me. As an only child he was to me what your sister was to you, no offense meant to her, on the contrary. So, that evening understandably, sleep was not coming easily. And I felt a little scared and asked to have my door open. To my horror I overheard my dad tell my mom, 'It was a horrible mess. Blood, flesh, fur all over the pavement. It was as if the truck had run over Blackie several times. In reality, first the truck hit him then several other vehicles drove over his dead body. I'll have nightmares about it.'

"If I had heard that my parents had been killed, it wouldn't have horrified me more. It was a one-two punch from which now, over sixty years later, I still haven't recovered. First, I learned my dog was never coming back; second, the edifice of my young life fell on top of me with a suffocating blow—my father had lied to me. That he didn't tell me the details of Blackie's demise I can understand, but he actually held out hope, almost swore to me, that my dog was coming back. To this day I believe that was a cowardly act. With the lie, he could stave off having to deal with the brunt of my grief and my first encounter with the reality of death. Nothing ever was the same for me after that. For one thing, I was constantly looking for evidence of him lying. I never again trusted a word he said to me. Nor did I ever share any of my secrets with him, not even the fact that I knew the truth about Blackie."

"Like all kids," I cut in, mostly just to say something to distract myself from my growing sense of guilt, "You learned fast that you had to take care of him before taking care of you."

"Cut the therapeutic crap, André." Gabe was always prone to outbursts. "The truth is that I didn't want to expose myself to more bullshit from him, including him attacking me in self-defense. No, I wasn't taking care of him. I was taking care of me by dodging his anticipated barrage of lies."

"Did you ever catch him lying again?" I asked.

"Literally hundreds of times." Now my friend's face turned deep red. I noticed the old rage brewing in him, a rage that I used to fear and that gave him severe headaches as far back as I could remember, at age eight or nine.

"He lied effortlessly and with the same ease as breathing. Once I overheard him lie to a customer about the quality of the leather being superb. I knew it was just the opposite. I said, 'Dad, why did you tell Mr. Szabo that the leather you wanted to sell him was above classification when you know it's next to garbage?' 'You know that and I know that, my boy, but he doesn't and that's what matters.' The sinister cynicism of his way of thinking and the message he sent to me at age ten was chilling. 'What about your teaching me to always tell the truth because the truth shall set me free?' I asked. 'The truth will set *you* free,' he relied with a cunning smirk on his face, 'but in business the truth shall set *me* bankrupt.'

"That sad day I learned the concept of a double standard and how it hurts. And you know what, André, have you ever wondered why I never got married or had kids? Well, to a great extent because I realized I was not going to be any better than him. Knowing first-hand how much his lies have hurt me, I didn't want to do the same to my kids or their mother. I never formed close bonds with anyone. In this way it was easier to tell the truth, on the one hand, and when I lied to people, they were definitely not my loved ones. This is still a double standard but I can live with it more at peace with myself."

That night, I had two very disturbing thoughts that kept me from falling asleep:

1. I've been not significantly better than Gabe's father in that I had lied to my children. Not about serious matters like life and death, but serious enough and untrue enough to be considered lies. And just as Gabe's dad, I too have been a hypocrite by expecting that they never tell a lie. Like all lies to one's children, they were uttered with the explicit purpose of making their lives easier, but in reality, they made my life easier, at least in the short run.

I was not above telling them that I'll buy a particular gift for them later when I've more time and money rather than telling them that I had no intention of ever buying the damned thing. (I must say, the more children I had, the easier that particular challenge became.) Or, I'd tell them that a particular friend couldn't sleep over because I wasn't feeling well when in fact I didn't want the kid over because I thought she was a pest. Worse, I'd tell them the next day that I would be home early enough for us to play or read together, knowing full well that I had too much work to do so. All of these lies were evidence of wimping out on the kids, of not having enough faith in them and me working through their disappointments. But mostly, in spite of all my beliefs and efforts, I didn't have enough respect for them. People you respect definitely deserve that you deal with them truthfully. And then, hopefully, you have enough integrity and inner strength to be able and willing to live with the consequences of having told the truth. Another version of lying to our children is, rather than telling them the truth, which makes us squirm, we tell them, "You won't understand it. I'll tell you when you're older." The implication is that, of course, by the time they're older they'll either have forgotten or will have learned the truth from someone else. An instance of that with younger children as in Gabe's case has to do with death and dying. Or leaving their mom for another woman, or is Dad drunk so often, etc.

Instead of playing your kid for an idiot, tell him the truth. The fact is that you don't want to tell not because he can't understand but because you're scared that he *will* understand it and will ask questions you don't want to have to face and answer. I suggest that if they are old enough to ask the question, they're also old enough to hear the answer expressed in age-appropriate language and keeping the concept simple. Try to avoid telling your young child that boys come from the cabbages and girls from roses. Or that the stork brings them. If they ask, even at age four, tell them that they come from Mom and Dad loving each other and that Dad plants the seed and Mom has the soil in her tummy to grow it into a baby. There are several age-appropriate films and books that can be immensely helpful. Don't worry that they have a grossed out or traumatized reaction to learning this way about how we really make babies. The truth will set them free. And excited about life. And they'll feel secure in the truth that they were created out of Mom and Dad's love for each other.

If you're really uncomfortable about telling a particular truth and you can't successfully dissipate the noise in your head about it, try talking it over with your partner, friends, parents, siblings, other potentially wise and trustworthy people such as educators, therapists, enlightened clergy, or if you're lucky, your mentor. And if you can't find a book to guide you through this maze, tell your child the truth. "Look, honey, I don't know how to talk to you about this so that it would work for you and for me. I'll have to give it a lot more thought and find a way to talk to you about this. I promise I'll work on it." And if she asks why you can't talk about it, be sincere: "Because children aren't the only ones who become shy about certain things. Or embarrassed or scared; or just plain confused. So are parents, and so am I. But I will work on it." And then keep your promise.

2. I said there were two thoughts that kept me from sleeping the night after my conversation about lying to children with

my old friend, Gabe. The second thought was that the topic of the conversation instigated by Gabe made me feel so squirmy that rather than first embracing the opportunity to set myself free by choosing to address my occasional lack of truthfulness, I wished that I hadn't reconnected with him. A cowardly thought, but it's the truth.

Since then, I worked it through and I've been facing my demons of falsehood. You who are at the beginning of your journey as a father, take my word for it, lying to your child is never a good option. Telling as much truth as she can developmentally process is. And stop at that.

CHAPTER 31

GET YOUR OWN DAMNED SCREWDRIVER!

"By the time I was five, my dad caught on to a really good thing," Marty told us one night when, once again, the group was revisiting the topic of dads. "Being the astute professor that I've always known him to be, he would have had to be deaf, blind, and clueless, which he wasn't, not to see that I worshipped at his feet. There was no question about it: for me, at that highly impressionable age, he could have given divinity lessons to God, and walking-on-water lessons to Jesus.

"For a while, he thought it was cute, as I learned from him later. He was even flattered by such unconditional adulation. His ego was so huge (or perhaps so puny) that he gladly accepted applause from any audience.

"Then one day, I believe, he had a bright idea. 'If this kid of mine is going to be under my feet anyway, he may as well pay the price of admission.' From that day on, I became his errand boy.

"'Marty, my boy, fetch me my paper, will you? That's my boy,' he'd say.

"'Marty, what good is the paper to me if I don't have my glasses? I believe I left them on my desk in my study. Be a good lad and bring them to me so I can finally read my paper before it becomes yesterday's paper or litter-box liner.

"'Marty, you know what would be great right now for both of us? A nice crunchy red apple. What do you think, boychik? I think you see my point. Now run along, my mouth is watering already.

"'Marty, I can't find my Mont Blanc pen, the one Mommy gave me for my birthday. That's my favorite. Would you be good enough and look for it in my study, it can't be too far. But I won't rest until I have in my hands. You're a good boy, I know I can count on you, trooper.

"'Marty . . . Marty . . . Marty . . .'

"I was only five but a bright, tuned-in five, a true son of my father. I loved him to pieces and I would have walked through fire for him, but let's face it, he was exploiting my love and respect for him and he didn't even tip me. When I first realized that he was using me, I was proud. I felt like I had grown in importance. My father, the world-famous professor had use for me. Others would have gladly just watched him sleep, but I, I could do things for him. Then, one day I overheard my mom tell my dad: 'Don't you think you're abusing Marty's enthusiastic father worship? You've made him go up and down four times just this evening.' 'Are you kidding me? He loves it. He'd run up and down forty-four times if I'd ask him to do that. Besides, it's a pretty good deal to have my personal sherpa. I don't see you breaking your neck trying to relieve your son. Don't worry, he loves it. He'd do it forever if he could.'

"There was a lot I didn't understand in what he was saying to my mom. For one thing, I didn't know the meaning of the word 'sherpa.' And for another, I sensed he was making fun of me. 'If Mom thinks he's not being fair to me, he is not.' I thought I could hear my heart crack. My heart was mocking me. Mom has always been the incarnation of fairness. She was onto him.

"First, I was devastated; then I was hurt and pissed off. Then I was just pissed off. I was five but I had my pride. Scared as I was, I knew I had to do something.

"For a few days, business was as usual: 'Marty get this. . . . Marty get that. . . . Hurry up, I don't have all day. . . . Marty where are you, can't I count on my boy anymore? . . . Marty . . . !'

"Then the day came when, in spite of my unconditional devotion to this man who was larger than large, I rebelled. I was watching my favorite cartoons on the TV in the family room in the basement when I heard him yell down from the third floor: 'Marty, I can't find my Philips screwdriver and I need it in a hurry. Be a good lad and bring it to me on the double!' I made believe I didn't hear him. In fact, I turned up the volume on the TV a bit.

"'Marty, are you deaf? I really need that screwdriver, now, not tomorrow!'

"I didn't budge.

"'Marty, for crying out loud, can't I count on you anymore?' I heard his voice from the second floor.

"'Get your own damned screwdriver, Dad!'

"I didn't know where that came from, but I sure couldn't believe that it would have been from my mouth. I thought the floor was going to open under my feet and would swallow me. I shook with fear but I was also happy. For one thing, I had never used the word 'damned' in front of my parents. And for another, I had no idea what kind of response I would get.

"'What did you say, Marty?' I heard my dad's voice. This time he was standing at the top of the basement steps. 'Is there something wrong? Couldn't you hear I was calling for you to bring me my Philips screwdriver? This TV is blasting, no wonder you couldn't hear me. So are you going to bring that screwdriver? I have my hands full.'

"'I said get your own damned screwdriver.' This time my voice was calm; I was not even afraid. I felt right.

"That day something broke in our relationship that wasn't fixed until thirty years later when he agreed to come to see André with me. There were no serious overt repercussions from my act of rebellion. He got his own screwdriver without a response. But that evening he didn't come in to say good-night. I wept. The next morning, before he left, he scratched my head as he always does in the morning and with a calm in his voice that felt like a chill he said: 'Don't you swear at me ever again. Understood, Martin Joshua Friedman?' He never called me by my full name when he was happy. And he stopped using me as his errand boy. I felt punished. 'Do you want me to get you something, Dad?' I asked one Sunday afternoon as he was reading his paper. 'An apple perhaps?' 'I want nothing from you, boy, I don't like to be cursed at.'

"From then on he didn't ask me for favors, but he manipulated me all my life one way or another—with money, gifts, jobs. He knew that I would never refuse because I needed his help, I thought, but more importantly, because I wanted to please him. I wanted to buy myself back into his good graces so that he would feel free to exploit me again. Those days were over. When he came to see André with me, I confronted him: 'You never forgave me for the one act of self-assertion in a childhood of adoration and respect. You took advantage of my feelings for you and then when I rebelled in the only way I knew (I saw it in a movie I saw on TV with you), you evicted me from your heart for three decades. Dirty pool, Dad, damned dirty pool. You owe me big, old man.' It took him about ten sessions, but eventually he threw in the towel: 'You're right, I was out of line, as was my dad when he did it to me, and I took it out on you. That was dirty pool indeed, and I am sorry. What can I do now?'

"'Bring me a bloody screwdriver, for crying out loud, that's what,' I said, feeling like a boulder was lifted from the pit of my stomach. 'I mean at the pub across the street.'"

What grabbed me about this story when I first heard it and then every time I thought about is the power games fathers play with their kids. We make our kids perform for us in front of our friends and clients, to make us look and feel proud about what a good little monkey we've raised and how obedient he is. We freak them out with scary stories and then we burst out laughing at their expense, or we tease them about their most vulnerable secrets. Or, as Marty's dad did, we turn them into our little slaves. Or we do all of the above and more. Why? Because we can. Because we take their love and devotion for granted. And because we're pissed off at our own fathers for having done the same to us or for not being around enough to even do that. Marty's dad's generation was not big on confronting their fathers even if they were still alive.

Please try to be mindful of this all-important fact: it is not your child's fault that your father didn't love you the way your child would like to be loved and at times is. It's not his job to make it all feel better. If you're pissed off at your old man, deal with it, as did Marty. And if your partner or anyone else signals to you that there is a chance that you are exploiting or otherwise maltreating your child, listen to them. Agree with them at least in principle or agree with the probability that they may have a point. Who can say with the conviction of Marty's dad that he is doing nothing, absolutely nothing hurtful to his child? Our partners may have too sensitive an antenna for picking up even the faintest act of insensitivity. But they are seldom entirely wrong. So consider it as a message to your unconscious. And the way we take responsibility for our unconscious acts of nastiness is by agreeing to pay more attention the next time and expressing appreciation for being told this time. In the case of Marty's dad, he could have easily remedied the situation by now and then offering to fetch Marty something or asking him if he minded at all doing the favor he was asked to perform. Chances are he would have said no regardless of how he felt, but it would have felt good to be asked.

Our children are on loan to us. It is paramount that we pass them on to a life in which they grow up in at least as good a shape as when they have first arrived. This includes, now and then, fetching our own damned screwdriver. Let's not communicate to our kids that what they are doing is of no significance, that what we do is always of utmost importance to safeguard world peace.

CHAPTER 32

GLAD, NOT SAD

I know a sad young man who is sad today because, as far back as he can remember, his dad had scorned him for being a little old man in a child's body. He was always quiet and shy, whereas his father wanted the child to lift him and his Holocaust survivor friends out of their own misery and depression.

I also know a sad young woman whose father put her on the card table as a young child and made her sing and dance naked for his poker buddies. In her own recollection, this began when she was three but according to her older brother she was even younger.

And I recall that from the time when I was four, my father would take me to his dentist, who then pretended that he was going to pull all my teeth. The two grown men would laugh uproariously at my terror. The entertainment ended when I broke down in tears. "You're a regular wet blanket," my father would say. "I don't know why I bother with you."

The distinction between being laughed *with* and being laughed *at* is subtle only for those doing the laughing. To the recipient it pounds like a hammer of disrespect, stunting spontaneity with each blow.

It is usually the parent who destroys a child's natural exuberance. One quick way to accomplish this is to show no recognition or respect for the child's unique sensitivities, treating him instead as a pawn, created for one's own pleasure and entertainment. A child might come to you proudly displaying a wooden toy assembled backwards, or he has invented a new game of non-hop hopscotch. You may not find these things particularly amusing or inventive, or you might just be in a bad mood or a person who cannot be lifted from his chronic depression. Whatever the reason, you have just deflated a child's exuberance. Now, repeat this ad nauseam and you will have succeeded in creating a sad and uninspired individual. Sad children may not survive to maturity, or else they become sad adults who produce sad children.

To avoid creating sad children, laugh with and not at your child, pay attention to his creativity and encourage it, and don't tell funny stories about him that make him feel the object of amusement and ridicule. And if you are sad and depressed, seek help and don't rely on your child to lift you up and make you complete again. Too many adult children I see in my practice live day to day with the guilt of being responsible for their parents' unhappiness.

Once, we took our young son Adrian to see the movie *Ghostbusters*, and in one of the scenes appeared a couple of Orthodox Jews. Adrian exclaimed, proud of his mastery of yet another big word: "Look, orthopedic Jews!" Here was one occasion where I failed to honor my own edict and laughed aloud, much to his consternation and embarrassment. However, this temporary setback only increased my vigilance.

While a father can try very hard to keep the incidence of ridiculing his kids close to zero, there are other misdemeanors of trespassing on a child's sensitivities. My daughter Eliana, when she was about six, was for some reason terribly embarrassed by public displays of affection. And I don't mean making torrid love on the porch. My wife and I noticed her discomfiture when we once hugged amorously in the kitchen.

For some reason, and short-circuiting all vigilance, I found this sufficiently entertaining to continue the habit on successive days when I came home from work and Eliana was around. After about half a dozen incidents the coin finally dropped. I realized I was doing something that I would have considered cruel if the perpetrator were my own father. I apologized to Eliana that very night. She confessed that she thought that for some reason I'd somehow turned against her and wanted to hurt her. She had never experienced anything like that from me before and she wondered what she'd done to lose my love.

I heartily recommend that you refrain from entertaining yourself at your kid's expense, however innocent you think your behavior might be. It's the child's interpretation that matters. Any feelings of disloyalty by one or both parents may have long-lasting impact.

If you think from these examples that I'm making too much of this, that I'm totally devoid of humor, please consider the child's perspective. Some kids seem to take to humor from day one. Others may take ten to fifteen years to develop a sense of humor, and some never do. Even when a child begins to develop a reasonable facsimile, the ability to laugh at herself is a completely separate talent, which a large percentage of humans never seem to acquire. Whether lack of humor is inherited or learned is a moot point. By personal observation, humorless individuals are invariably blessed with humorless parents.

The good thing (or bad thing) is that your children in due time will likely mirror your own sense of humor. If you avoid crass or cruel jokes and do not enjoy other people's crass and cruel jokes, the chances are that eventually your child will not find them funny either. If you allow yourself to express the full gamut of emotions you possess without trampling on your kids' sensitivities, you can be sure that your kid will reflect them all back at you, though not necessarily on your time schedule.

My rule of thumb: although children know how to have fun and are often funny, they may not appreciate the adults' sense of humor. Their contribution to lightening our load is their contagious joy of just being alive.

CHAPTER 33

I HAVE NO CHOICE BUT . . .

Although we say we believe in free will, face to face with a little child no more than three or four, many a father will blithely exclaim: "Young man, you leave me no choice but to . . ." (insert your favorite dreaded consequence). My question is, how does this little ragamuffin take away your freedom of choice? Are we really talking about choice here, or merely replaying a soundtrack from our own past, perhaps recorded in our dad's voice. Listen. Can you hear him?

Do we really think for one moment that our child will understand the meaning of such a pronouncement any better than we did when we were his age? Will the result be any different? I don't know about you, but the only effect I remember is a sense of powerlessness. "Young man, you leave me no choice." What twisted logic! Not only was I being punished for something or other, but I was also being accused of forcing my father to punish me in spite of his better judgment.

Although with our adult brains we can work it through and may even make some sense of it, there's not a chance in a million that a child would. Two of my daughters, independently, and at different times, confronted me with the absurdity of "you leave me no choice." Eliana, a courtroom lawyer at twelve, once locked horns with me over the choice of school she wanted to attend. After repeated arguments on both sides, I decided to invoke parental authority, using among others the phrase "You leave me no choice."

She was right, of course. I was too worn down, going on autopilot, never imagining for a moment that the phrase might be challenged. Since I'd never really thought what it actually meant, I was chagrined that it became the subject of scrutiny. Surely, if someone with a gun had said to me at that instant: "You have thirty seconds to come up with ten choices or you'll never see your child again," I would have had no trouble at all, and with time to spare.

Cybèle, my first-born, being a mature fourteen, was even more direct in her response. She first burst out laughing, then, shaking her head, said: "Dad, this is the dumbest thing you've ever said to me."

"And why is that?" I asked, innocently.

"What if I said to you, 'Dad, in view of my repeated requests for a bigger allowance, which were denied, you leave me no choice but to sell drugs at school'?"

My mentor Harvey once said: "When outclassed, retreat gracefully." The same man in a more serious vein also said, "When you think you have no choice, find three." We all know there is always a choice, even if it's not the choice we prefer.

Rather than blaming our kids for what we intend to do to them, we should at least express ourselves in a way that's understandable and makes sense. Otherwise, we're just firing a toxic soundbite, a missile aimed at our children and generations to come.

When my child does something I don't wish to tolerate, and I'm momentarily disinclined to engage in a round of mental gymnastics, I try to get across that I mean business, that my decision stands, and that we shall get into the nitty-gritty later, at a convenient time. It's a good idea to actually make an appointment. You would be surprised how easy and effortless most follow-up discussions become once robbed of the intensity of the initial confrontation.

More often than not, your child, come the appointed time, will have lost interest in pursuing the matter further. The reason is of course that she knew that you were right all along but was trying to get her own way regardless.

At other times, she might feel genuinely wronged. If so, your dialogue can become a rare and wonderful opportunity to exchange views with your child about something very relevant to today, yet without the emotional charge that often nixes any attempts at rational communication. She will have an opportunity to restate her case (so will you but keep it brief) and perhaps offer additional arguments that may alter the outcome and even cause you to revoke your decision. Remember to keep the discussion brief and resist the temptation of branching out into other items of contention. You want to make this a productive encounter, so that it has a chance of being repeated. Don't browbeat your child so that she leaves the room discouraged. Give a little, even if you hadn't meant to, so that you both can hold your heads high. And leave the room together so it doesn't seem to her like an appointment with the headmaster.

To communicate effectively, we must: witness, empathize, and validate. This formula works not only with your child but also with your boss, your partner, your neighbor, and maybe even the tax examiner. If you practice it to fluency, you'll find it eases your life considerably by deescalating conflict before it blooms into confrontation. *Listen* to everything the child wants to say to support her point of view or in her defense (even if it's something you've heard many times and has never worked before). Acknowledge the child's indignation as valid from her perspective. And tell her that you understand her point of view and that you're sorry it has come to this difference of opinion. You may be unpopular for a while, but your child knows that you care. Ultimately, when the noise dies down, caring is what matters the most.

CHAPTER 34

SPARE THE ROD, SPARE THE CHILD, PART 1

It's hot, damn hot out here in the streets of Toronto today. If it makes any difference, the weather bureau just informed us that with the humidity, we're at 113° F. It's hotter in Canada than in parts of Africa. While we might welcome this temperature in the middle of winter, it is definitely inelegant to be sweltering in Toronto, a city that prides itself on moderation.

Why am I dwelling on the weather? Because I've just witnessed an exchange between a father and son, not older than four. The man's face dripped like a leaky faucet, his muscular physique ready to explode with ill-contained frustration. His son was giving vent to his discomfort by demanding (and demanding) an ice cream cone from a nearby vendor.

"No ice cream for you, you little bum," yelled the outraged dad. "You can pull that number with your mother but not with me."

"But I am a good boy and I want my ice cream! You promised."

"Not now you're not," retorted the dad. "Any more of this and I'll give you a smack you won't forget anytime soon."

The child began whimpering silently. He looked wounded and betrayed, none of it making sense to him. His dad looked at his son and lost it. He delivered the whack he'd promised. (At least he'd kept one promise that day.) Their bus pulled up and he dragged the wailing child into the vehicle. "Shut up or the driver will throw us out," I overheard him say as the doors closed.

It would be almost comforting to believe that scenes like this only happened in extreme weather conditions.

Once again a controversy is raging about physical punishment. For many years, beginning with the postwar peace movement, typified by Dr. Spock, educators tried to best each other in the vehemence of their condemnation. In the last ten years or so, voices have re-emerged sanctioning a limited use of force on (against) a child. I think I have just betrayed my bias. I believe it won't be a surprise to any of my readers that I stand firmly on the side of nonviolence regardless of its "justification."

The Bible is firmly in support of corrective action by physical force, parents having the right and obligation to spank an errant child in accord with their standards and personal choice. A whole book could be written about punishment, but I will spare you the diatribe by narrowing down the subject to a measly two chapters.

How many times have you been told as a kid, or have you heard adults tell their kids, "That's not fair. Why don't you pick on someone your own size? How would you like it if I started pushing you around?" Yet the same grownup has no problem spanking his kids or (where legally permissible) other people's kids.

I propose to you fathers, because I'm speaking mostly to fathers although women are by no means exempt, that you hit your kid because you can get away with it—which makes you nothing but a bully. Not only that, but you are also creating a bully in your own image. As soon as the child reaches your size or bigger, you will no longer be so eager to "teach him a lesson." In fact, if you have mistreated him enough, he will turn on you, just like a mistreated dog turns on its master.

It's in the father's best interest to teach his child that to raise his hand to a parent is not only disrespectful but also a mortal sin. The way to accomplish this is by showing the way—by respecting the child's body and mind. A child raised in this way may grow to a towering height but will never strike his parent, not even if deliberately provoked.

If you beat your child when he is little and stop before he enters his teens, he may not strike you when he grows up, but he'll likely save it up for later, dumping his shit-load on his own kid, who then does the same to the next generation. Call this the curse that keeps on cursing or, in Alice Miller's words, "the multi-generational cycle of abuse."

And abuse it is. Don't let anyone convince you otherwise, mostly against younger children, who are the most defenseless. Parents or educators who advocate and/or practice corporal punishment achieve nothing of an educational nature. The most common outcomes can be summed up as follows:

1. Fear of the parent later becomes fear of all authority, especially male, or worse, a pervasive state of fear, permeating everything in life.

2. Children, who know that regardless of what they do or how they behave, they will be struck, conclude that they have zero influence over their fate. The only available alternative is to deaden their feelings so as to make the pain tolerable. As a side benefit they also achieve a sort of personal victory by denying some of their tormentor's pleasure in inflicting the pain. Self-numbing often manifests later in life as an inability to feel any kind of physical or emotional well-being or pleasure. The other shoe is always about to drop.

3. Children who endure a steady diet of corporal punishment or "loving correction" with rod, stick, or belt either engage in an internal, passive rebellion or fight back with deceit, lies, and vindictiveness. Whether they act out passively or not, both patterns of behavior are destructive as well as self-destructive.

"My dad would spank me, hit me, strap me, you name it," Veronica, thirty years old, told me just a couple of days ago. "It went on until I was about fourteen. I had fantasies of pushing him under a car or off the balcony of our high-rise apartment. But I didn't. Not because I was scared but because I also loved him, crazy as it may sound. At times he could be really sweet and supportive and all that. I began to steal from him when I was about ten, just stuff I had no use for, out of revenge. I would hide his razor, his car keys, and his tennis racquet. Then, I got smart. I began to dip into his cash, a couple of dollars here and there, then more. He suspected me but I became a super-ingenious liar. My mom knew though and told me I deserved to be smacked because I was a liar and a thief. But I became a liar and a thief as a way to balance things. You strike where I hurt and I strike where you hurt. The one thing I learned is that my mom was no more in my corner than my dad."

I remember Elizabeth, who sublet from us when my first-born was two. We took Elizabeth with us to the swimming pool on a hot day in Southern California. We were all delighted to be in the cool water, except Elizabeth. She refused to come in. That evening I had a talk with her. After a lot of silence and false starts, she blurted out, "It's like this, André. As far back as I can remember, my father beat us almost everyday. Some kids were lucky they got it from their dad only on Fridays. But he got drunk more so we got it all the time. He beat me with whatever was handy while ranting about how it was for my own good because I was rotten. I was too wimpy and scared to be anything but a piece of furniture. Then by the time I was six I trained myself not to pay attention to my body since it was mostly hurting. Since then, I feel safer and more peaceful if I pay absolutely no attention to my body."

"Is that why you didn't go into the pool?" I asked.

"Yes," she replied without emotion. "I don't feel the heat. If I'd gone into the water it would have felt really good. I would rather feel nothing than good. Behind the good is the pain."

Elizabeth's words had the ring of ultimate authority.

CHAPTER 35

SPARE THE ROD, SPARE THE CHILD, PART II

I have yet to meet an adult reminiscing about his childhood, or for that matter a child, who would admit candidly, "I'm grateful to my dad for hitting me. By doing so, he taught me the difference between right and wrong, kindness toward others, and most of all, love and respect for myself." The most I ever heard people owning up to is that they hadn't been traumatized for life. It hadn't corrected them, but it hadn't destroyed them either.

What I do see quite often is the story of abused children who in turn became child beaters themselves, for whom hitting is a given. The standard of reference is the degree of violence they were subjected to. "She shouldn't complain. I got it a lot worse from my old man." Some of his kids get more, some less.

At times, I'm tempted to feel empathy for these severely abused former children, who need understanding in therapy as much as their victims do, but all I can muster is compassion, and I tell them that. As they begin to see their behavior in a broader context, they begin to recognize the cycle of abuse that they have been trapped in. I have witnessed complete turnarounds. The successful converts are often extremely grateful and occasionally even become dedicated to stopping all child violence, some to the point of becoming advocates of child rights in the neighborhood, sending me new offenders as potential clients.

How can you not be moved to compassion by the sight and sound of a child in pain, looking terrified, betrayed, defeated? How can you not stop dead in your track and tell yourself: this is not an option. No child deserves to be hurt regardless of what she'd done. No lesson is worth this price. *There is another way.*

How can you continue beating your kid, look in the mirror, and still consider yourself a decent human being? If anyone else raised a hand or belt to your son or daughter, you'd do whatever necessary to protect them. Why is it different when you do it?

The reason so many parents feel free to strike their children is their unwarranted assumption of ownership. We can do what we want with our stereos or bowling balls because they're ours. We own them. I can only reiterate: we do not own children. Children are loaned to us for safekeeping, care giving, and loving. From the very beginning they are individuals who have sole possession of their individual lives, with all rights and privileges afforded to adults. During the period of the loan, while we help them become self-sufficient, they teach us about ourselves. Because of their presence in our lives we have the opportunity to fine-tune our best qualities: generosity, compassion, altruism, affection, and creativity, and as a result our lives become immeasurably enriched. We give and get love, joy, adventure, happiness, and occasional sorrow. We learn to think beyond ourselves, about the world, as something more than a playground for our immediate gratification. These are the things that children do for us. However, very often, indeed continuously, we need to remind ourselves that we don't own them.

I recall my wife's bewilderment when early in her career she worked for the Children's Aid Society. She was once dispatched to investigate a complaint about a child being physically abused by his father and the mother not intervening. When she arrived at the house, the angry father told her to stop sticking her nose in other people's private business, that he had the right to raise his child according to how he saw fit and that no one had any f— right telling him what he could or could not do. After all, this was his child, not theirs. And to make the situation more frustrating, the mother was fully on his side.

I have not the slightest doubt that these parents were victims of abuse. Some of us, or most of us (depending on the age group), were also beaten as children. Just because we were also beaten, and so were our fathers and their ancestors, does that mean that it's okay? After all we're happy to drive cars, fly planes, watch TV, and speak on cell phones, none of which was available to our forefathers. Just because something has been forever doesn't rule out new ideas' being superior.

We never hit our children when we are at peace with the world. We lose control and lash out when we're frustrated, exasperated, indignant, hurt, let down, anxious, angry, or otherwise not well in our skin.

It may seem to help to vent on our kid. But is it the kid who is responsible? The same behavior draws no attention whatsoever when you're on top of your game. But today you have been told that the project you've been working on for six months was being scrapped, that your rent check bounced, and your doctor phoned to say you've got herpes; and on top of it all this little bastard of a kid had to choose this day to spill his Coke, plug the toilet, or crank the volume to the max watching his Barney video. So now you're ready to really give it to him.

Rewind. You just got an unexpected sizable bonus for the project to which you've devoted your last six months, your favorite baseball team won the World Series, and your wife greeted you at the doorstep wearing nothing but her trench coat. Put all of Junior's offenses into this context. Are you likely to really give it to him? In other words, it's all about *you* and nothing about her. This is the "kicking the dog" syndrome. When the dog happens to be your child (or even if it's your dog, but that's another subject), all red lights should be flashing in your head.

Then there are religious communities that claim immunity from the mores of society at large, invoking the teachings of their sacred beliefs to support the use of violence toward children, while calling it an act of responsible love.

I read in the August 3 editorial in the Toronto *Globe and Mail* newspaper about the showdown between the Children's Aid Society and the Church of God in a small community in southern Ontario. The society removed seven children from their homes because the parents refused to promise that they would desist beating their children with sticks. Their authority: the Book of Proverbs (King James Version) wherein is written, "he that spareth the rod hateth his son." Elsewhere, Proverbs also encourage parents to use a stick or a bundle of sticks to drive "foolishness far from a child," and that "beating your child will not kill him, the contrary it will deliver his soul from hell."

How can one argue with the authority of the Bible? Or with those who take those words literally but who at the same time break other teachings concerning right and wrong, such as lying on income tax returns, living a life motivated by greed, and cheating on their spouses? Clearly this path is not likely to be lit by the cool light of reason.

When a father strikes his child, the intention doesn't matter. You can be sure that your child has the same nerve fibers, muscles, bones, and skin as you do. If somebody runs you over because they were rushing to the hospital, your injuries won't heal any faster than if you had been struck by a careless driver. Can you recall having been taught one single lesson by being hit that you would not have learned by some more user-friendly approach? If your faith teaches you compassion, that also includes compassion toward your child.

If you find this all too confusing and wish to seek clarification from the legal system, you will be disappointed and no less confused. At least in Ontario, the Criminal Code doesn't disallow corporal punishment "if the force doesn't exceed what is reasonable under the circumstances." But elsewhere in the Code, according to the *Globe and Mail* editorial, assault is defined as any act that applies force to another person without that person's consent. Would a child ever consent, meaning that a child is not a person?

In short, according to this law, reasonable force may be applied to a child if the situation warrants it. Gone is the concept that willfully afflicting pain without consent is an act of assault. Gone are the notions of empathy and wisdom. (Not that one expects empathy and wisdom in the Criminal Code.) How often would people admit to using unreasonable force? And what magnitude of punishment is justifiable when the child needs to be disciplined in order to save her from the snares of "Satan"? Here, the law invites child beaters to continue their abusive practices within reason—an oxymoron if I ever heard one!

Section 43 of the Criminal Code of Canada represents the prevailing yardstick in assessing the criminality of using force to discipline children, under the title "Correction of Child by Force." Can you think of a few adults who could use a little correction? Then, why not use force on adults as well, as they do in Singapore?

The Supreme Court, in a specific judgment, determined that customs of contemporary Canadian society are the appropriate standards in the conduct of these matters. Given that there is no such a thing as a Canadian society, which segments of that society do we use as the guide?

If it is to be the society in which the Church of God is the provider of divine inspiration, then the members have acted in accord with their society's norm. So the same child, who by good fortune was born in another community, would not be receiving the beating. For Pastor Hilderbrand, loving his children includes "corporal punishment with something other than our hands . . . a flexible instrument such as a leather belt." If this is an instance of love, I shudder to think what his anger may lead him to do? Chopping off a hand? Putting out an eye? Castration? Provided that these practices are within his community's customs, why not?

But don't we have a duty to protect the absolute rights of a child in the same spirit that nations can be made to answer to an international court?

Let's be real. Your child, just as mine or anyone else's, will on occasion do her best to push our buttons. This is the way it is. She would give me cause for worry if she were always a goody-two-shoes. Children are made to provoke our instincts. It's their job to make us deliberate on our own values, given that we have probably not had occasion to re-examine them since they were molded in our youth. But at other times, they may be signaling to us that something is not going well in their universe, when it is up to us to make that determination. A child does not yet possess the intellectual or emotional means to tell us which it is. Her acting out is a generic call for help. In these instances, while your urge may be to kill, I would recommend that you remove yourself from her presence, take a shower, run around the block a few dozen times, and later discuss things with your partner.

Consider this. I promised you that there was a better way, a way based upon revising our concept of who we are in relation to our children. I hope you have accepted my contention that our children are not our possessions, but if you haven't yet, I have not abandoned all hope in you. I would still like you to consider a different way of looking at your child.

The decent, respectful, and democratic way to walk the journey with another person is side by side, especially if the other person is someone you love. You should not rush ahead and let her trail behind you or let her run too far ahead. Imagine you're walking the journey with your child through a maze where there are many traps and detours as well as the occasional scary apparition. Your role is that of a guide. You want your child to emerge safe and sound at the other end so that one day in the future she may guide her children safely through a similar maze.

Now stop to think for a moment and consider how your relationship with your child differs from the one I have just proposed.

For one, the word "punishment" becomes obsolete. You can substitute phrases such as "limit setting" or "constructive guidance," which are more appropriate to your new role. After all, the little tyke does not know right from wrong; she is merely expressing her understanding of the world in her limited scope. Coming down heavy on your child is totally inappropriate in this context. Even when an adult appears before the courts, the prosecution must prove that the defendant knew the nature of the crime at the time the crime was being committed.

Yes, *there is another way*! When you find yourself losing your temper and about to strike out, think of yourself as a guide walking side by side with your child and not as a parent. This is your journey and you are in it together.

CHAPTER 36

PAIN HURTS

"By the time you get married, you won't remember," my dad used to say whenever I got hurt or complained about some injury. Or when I had to go to the dentist, or before a vaccination, or when I got a long wooden splinter in my heel.

Who doesn't remember being told, "Come on, don't be such a wimp (sissy, chicken, baby). This is nothing; it's just a little scratch. So what's a little blood? Okay, if you won't listen to reason you'll go to your room until you calm down. *If you don't stop crying this minute, I'll give you something to really cry about!*"

The aim of all these incredibly wise parental interventions is to invalidate the child's experience of hurt. The parent is really saying, "I don't believe you're really hurting. You're exaggerating the whole scene to get my attention. So what I'm going to do is threaten you enough that you'll be more scared of the consequences of my anger than whatever it is you are feeling right now."

Young children don't know how to be stoic. They haven't yet learned the art of overriding their feelings with their brains, nor do I think it wise they should. They have ample time when they grow older, when they can exercise a choice about what to override and what needs airing. Parental stunting of feelings at an early age carried on long enough and persistently enough is likely to shut down feelings en masse.

Feelings can shut down after a long period of provocation, once the child realizes he can get back at the parent by not showing any emotion when he is being punished.

Take my client Fred, the product of parental abuse of a fairly common sort: alcoholic mother and absent father, who when present believed in corporal punishment. I had been seeing Fred on and off for about three years in the mid-nineties. During that time he'd roller coasted through at least four relationships. Fred related, that at age seven, having gotten ten lashes with a belt, he turned around and looked his father in the eye and asked without emotion whether he was done beating him. The father, stunned, could only mutter yes, to which my client said, thank you, and walked upstairs. His father stopped beating him pretty much from then on—but at what price?

Or an even more insidious outcome is that the child buries his feelings and ends up agreeing with his parents that he is bad—and that bad boys have bad feelings! Once feelings have been shut down, they are hard to awaken again.

"If you stop crying, I'll get you some chocolate ice cream. . . . Come quick! Look what happens when I wind up this little truck and turn it upside down. Whirr. Isn't it funny? . . . I'm gonna get you, Charlie Brown. Mommy's gonna get you . . ." (as she stomps her feet in mock pursuit).

What we're doing here is a bit subtler. We're substituting ice cream, or playacting, or humor, or some other distraction to veer away the focus from the painful episode to something pleasurable. Of course, we adults are experts at this type of sublimation. We do it all the time with booze or pills or sex. So why not teach our youngsters as soon as possible?

We don't do it out of malice, of course. All parents squirm to see their child in pain. We would do anything to make it go away, the quicker the better. Most parents experience the child's pain more than he does. His toothache hurts us more, as does a scraped knee, especially in the days when iodine was dabbed on the wound. But for a few, the screaming child is nothing more than a disturbance, a nuisance, and an unpleasant cacophony. As I said elsewhere in this book, my father was not a bad man. He too had parents who despite their best intentions didn't succeed in parenting very well. My father's concern, when I hurt myself (as it seemed to me much later in life), was that I not disturb the silence of his depression.

The truth is that very often what we need to do as parents is to witness with empathy the child's experience. We pick him up and gently hug him, remembering that much of his distress is fright. Then, if he is old enough to talk, we listen, *we listen*, to his account of what happened and how it happened and how much it really hurts, thereby validating that what the child feels is appropriate. The child is not a sissy even if he may seem so in adult eyes. He is just a child and behaving like a child. A child is not a fully formed human being; he's in the process of becoming one, under our tutelage. He deserves our support and respect, not ridicule.

Having witnessed and validated the child's experience we track where the child seems to be going and follow him there. The point I'm trying to make is that it is not the best approach to short-circuit the child's natural mechanism for dealing with hurt, even if it represents the fastest reduction in the noise level. Since hurt is inevitable, every child needs to prepare for handling it in his own way, on his way to adulthood, when the parents can no longer function as shock absorbers or are no longer around.

The situation is quite similar when your young child is only scared and not actually hurt. Whether he is afraid of the dark, of a sudden noise, an impending dentist appointment, changing schools, or a myriad of other causes, don't trivialize it by telling your child that you've lived through something a lot scarier. Refrain from a demeaning comment like "It's nothing. When I was your age, I had to walk four miles to school in a snowstorm."

First of all, when your child is frightened, he doesn't care about your childhood, and rightfully so. Second, you were never his age because you were your age. The apparent similarity in chronology is totally irrelevant. Fear is unique and nonduplicable. Because fear is so compelling, it forces us to be one-track-minded, to the exclusion of any fables we might concoct. There is always room for these, long after the event.

The witness/validate/empathize formula works best. The experience of fear is real and authentic. Feel free to support it without reservation. What the child is scared of is another story. After validating and empathizing with the feeling, you can address objectively and in realistic terms the source of the fear. In addition to having to cope with the anticipated pain, parents are inclined to saddle the child with the guilt of not living up to their expectations.

Don't even suggest that getting a needle doesn't hurt because he won't believe it, nor is it true. In fact, it may erode your credibility for the next time. It's more honest to tell him that it hurts for a moment and quickly goes away, something much less painful than a bee sting.

When your child is scared of the dentist, tell him that it hurts less than a needle in your arm and that, after that, the instruments make funny buzzing noises. You could also offer to stay with him for moral support, but better clear it with the dentist first. I've been told that many children's dentists welcome this.

Every child, at one time or another is freaked by an ominous shadow on the wall of his room after lights out. I used to tell my kids that I understood that they were really scared and that the shadows were definitely real. Turning the light on and off a few times helped to explain the fleeting nature of the shadows and where they were coming from. After all, "there is nothing there in the dark that is not there in the light."

By now you may have guessed that I am not a proponent of the bite-your-lip school of thought. One of the important side benefits of not talking your child out of his experience is that it allows you to relive your own, from the point of view of the child but with adult minds. This builds towards a sensitive communion with the child. Biting our lips merely gives us sore lips and no side benefits.

CHAPTER 37

DON'T BITE YOUR CHILD

Earlier today, Cybèle, my first-born, and I were munching on our respective sandwiches in my office. Since she had done a fair bit of word processing and editing on this book so far, she knows its contents fairly well. I asked her if she could think of any significant incident that I have not yet addressed. She thought for a moment, looked at the ceiling, and as if she saw an image on screen, her eyes lit up. "What about the time you bit Tristana in Mexico?" she asked looking me in the eye as if to say: "You and I both know this is a must. Bite the bullet and go for it."

With her usual incisive intuition and intelligence, she saw right through me. In this book, I disclosed a lot of hard truths, but this one I somehow just didn't think of. How strange. . . . So, since I tend to advise others that the best antidote to the dark side is to move it to the light side, that is, exposure, I must do the same.

May 1974. Cybèle is eight; Tristana is nearly two. We are spending half a year on my postdoctoral fellowship at the University of California in San Diego. It's a bright and warm Sunday morning. I put Tristana into a comfortable sundress while Cybèle picks a similar one for herself. Bear with me, these details are important. I decide to drive down to the border town of Tijuana, at that time and perhaps still the cesspool of Mexico. The streets are teeming with people—tourists ogling the curios, haggling for bargains, pulling and shoving. The local hucksters push expertly through the crowds, offering pseudo-bargains, as I keep one hand on my back pocket. I hold on to Tristana's hand a little tighter.

Tristana is a regular live wire, curious and impetuous, the individualist she was to become all her life. I have less concern for Cybèle, who is older, mellower, and wiser, sticking close by my side. We pass by a doorway that attracts Tristana's attention. An old man is making faces at her. She is fascinated, while I'm getting alarmed. My suspicious mind tells me that this man could be dangerous. Sure enough, he is gesturing to my little girl to come to him, holding a colorful object in his hand. "Just stay with me, sweetheart, okay?"

I say. In reply, she tears her hand out of my grip and takes off toward the old man. "Tristana, stop, stop!" She doesn't hear me. She's mesmerized by the object in his hand. She reaches the doorway before I can catch her. The man scoops her up and disappears into the house. My heart leaps into my throat. I can't even scream, overwhelmed with rage and terror.

With petrified Cybèle in tow, I dash through the doorway as if it were the gate of hell, preparing for some spectacle of horror. Instead, I find myself in a courtyard full of people, full of kids dressed in their Sunday best, playing laughing, eating, and drinking, happy to be where they are.

It was a birthday party, while the messenger from hell turned out to be a gentle grandfather, who thought it would be a good idea to introduce my little girl to all these other kids. But at that moment, fired on adrenaline, I felt like strangling him. Instead, I picked up my Tristana, grabbed her tightly, and sank my teeth into her shoulder. She didn't breathe for the longest time, her mouth frozen open. Then she let out a scream of pain and outrage to rattle the dead. Cybèle was digging her nails into my arm trying to bring me back from the edge of near-insanity. She had never seen me very angry, let alone out of control.

She has heard me lecture her hundreds of time about the importance of talking things through rather than physically hurting someone. She has also heard from me as many times reassurances that my children were safe with me. And here I go taking a chunk out of Tristana's tiny shoulder. It takes but a minute for my teeth marks to emerge, accusingly pointing the finger at the savage beast that I have become because I couldn't tame my emotional overload.

Need I say that this was the end of that happy outing for the three of us that sunny afternoon? Tristana was in obvious pain and disarray. I got some ice to soothe the physical pain but there was nothing I could do to make her feel calmer and safe enough. She was crying for her mommy inconsolably, which she never did when she was me. Cybèle didn't know whether to be scared or feel sorry for her sister or what. It just made no sense to her all of a sudden. That actually was my own experience of myself. Later, over the years, when I recounted the incident to benevolent friends, in their kindness and solidarity with me they attempted to let me off the hook: "You were terrified with fear for her, she deliberately disobeyed you, so obviously you got really angry; you were in an unsafe place, so of course you'd lose your usual cool. It's not like you were a habitual child abuser; to the contrary, you're the safest and most gentle father we've ever known."

I did appreciate their efforts to empathize with me. I, on the other hand, had and still have a different perspective. No matter what feelings fuelled my act of violence, I was and am always responsible for behaving in a way that is safe for others, especially if they happen to be children. I work with a lot of men who, as a consequence of what they perceive rightly or wrongly as provocation, hit or otherwise physically or emotionally assault others. Most often they start out by feeling victimized: "She left me no choice but . . ." or "She made me so angry that I just couldn't control myself," or, "He knows how to push my buttons and when they are pushed watch out." The common denominator in all these different ways of accounting for the reasons of their acts of violence, and my biting my daughter is the basic fact: one way or another, I am responsible for dealing with my anger, rage, frustration, or fear in a way that doesn't feel like vomiting bile all over the other. If I don't let the other push my buttons, no matter what he does, I will not lash out. If I had had this concept clearly and irrevocably etched into my consciousness prior to the Tijuana assault, I would have dealt with Tristana's childlike rambunctiousness in a way that would have excluded me biting her. As such, what I did was totally inadmissible, and to this day, some twenty-six years later, I can see the expression of terror frozen on my little girl's face because I was not on top of my reaction. I have apologized to her numerous times, she has forgiven me numerous times, and still, I know that on that particular day, I acted in a way that shattered my illusions about being a man above violence.

The best self-defense against a hair-trigger is slowing down one's reactions. To do so, you need to talk to yourself as if you were a wise older man who is in your corner. Ask yourself: "Is this really important? Will it be important a year from today? If not, then it's not important now either. Is this about me or about the other? If I react from emotions, I may get into trouble. Am I willing to risk hurting somebody I love? Am I willing to hurt myself by getting charged with assault and battery? What do I really need here?" If you pay attention to that wise voice, essentially what you'll be doing is inserting thinking between an event and your emotional reaction. Rational thinking is always more likely to be your friend than emotional reaction.

What should I have done instead of biting my daughter? When I saw that she was well and not in danger, I could stay there with the kids and enjoy the festivity to which the old man invited us in his crude manner. If not, just take Tristana by the hand or pick her up and calmly tell her that we'll be going now, everything is just fine. And then later, perhaps at home, tell her that it's important to stay with Daddy in a strange place to make sure that we don't get separated. Then reassure her again that everything is fine. With this kind of benevolent debriefing, everything *will* be fine.

CHAPTER 38

THE SHAME OF IT ALL

Some parents start shaming their child really early, as if to beat the rush. "You can't start soon enough showing them who's the boss" (meaning who's the slave), one dad instructed me in a playground long ago, on seeing me "reprimand" my daughter Tristana at age four in quiet, loving tones. She had muscled her way in front of his son on the slide.

I squatted next to my daughter so that I could touch her and speak to her eye to eye about the incident. "How would you like it if someone pushed you aside when it was your turn?"

She replied with a prolonged silence, staring into space.

"Well?" I insisted.

"I don't know."

I looked at her quizzically. She then looked in the general direction of the boy, and then looked down on her toes to make sure they wiggled okay. "I'm sorry," she said softly.

I gave her a peck on the cheek and said, "I'd like you to promise you'll try to remember that everybody has to take turns. It's much better when people wait their turn and don't bully others. Do you think you should tell him you're sorry?"

She ran off and muttered something to the boy, who seemed to pay no attention whatsoever, absorbed in some other activity. Then she cut to the big tire in the middle of the playground, happy and carefree. Young children don't dwell on trivia as adults do. They are now-oriented, which is fortunate because it allows us license to make the occasional mistake. It's only when we hammer in mistakes with constant repetition that children absorb the message and their life alters course.

"Soft solutions," rumbled the boy's dad with scorn. "They don't work with kids, trust me. I'm a second grade teacher and I have three kids of my own. If it were my kid, I'd have grabbed him by the ear. 'How do you like that, you little monster? Who the hell do you think you are? You should be ashamed of yourself for picking on someone smaller.'"

Kids are naïve but not stupid. The little boy might have been thinking, "He seems to be saying I should pick on somebody bigger and get creamed. Now, here is a wise lesson: pick on a giant so he can pulverize me!"

Natural competitiveness, self-centeredness, impatience, and simple reorientation of children don't deserve the accompaniment of shaming. Shaming implies there is something intrinsically wrong with you, and no kid should ever be reduced to that conclusion. Children do not develop empathy until about eight years of age. Empathy requires one to put himself into the other's place, an impossibility until certain circuits get hooked up in the brain. It is completely illogical and shortsighted to judge toddlers by how we would behave under similar circumstances.

When I was a child, to be Jewish was shameful and sometimes fatal. My father, to teach me how to protect myself, told me to avoid Christian kids like the plague because they all hated Jews. True enough. Encounters with anti-Semitic kids tended to be bloody, driving the lesson home. Once, after scarlet fever had sent me to the hospital, my dad brought me an orange, a rare and much envied delicacy in Budapest, especially for a poor family. The same day, someone stole it while I napped. When I reported it to the nurse, she responded, "Jews don't need oranges, they need a kick in the pants." The kids on the ward, as if on cue, proceeded to chase me around, acting out the nurse's observation all the while laughing uproariously. How did that make me feel? Like a piece of shit— the universal response to shaming.

Every time we shame a child, instead of helping her grow we cut her down to size. Have you ever seen a kid just after her parent blasted her with a deadly putdown? You can actually see the face blanch and body thin out, almost hear the heart stop. What she really hears beyond "What good are you, you stupid girl?" is that her parents wouldn't miss her if she vanished. No wonder the abused child becomes silent and shrinks to fit the allotted space, the space she thinks she deserves. You can bet your bottom dollar that one day, when she exceeds her tolerable quota, she'll become difficult to manage, and later, a financial asset to her psychotherapist, liquor supplier, or coke dealer. In the meantime, her childhood will be riddled with all kinds of insecurities and general misery.

When you really think about it, and I hope you will, what is your purpose of putting down your child? Are you just satisfying some inner need because your life hasn't met up to your expectations? Do you really hate her enough to steal her sun? Are you merely replaying an old tune you learned from your parents? It was good enough for me, so . . . Have you forgotten how it felt when your dad let you know in so many ways that you were nothing special? When you say, "Who the hell do you think you are?" is it because you really think that she is a nobody, a nothing? Does it mean that you feel, "I sure as hell am nothing but a big zero and you're no better"? As in my father's words, "One day you'll end up on the gallows, you'll see!"

I heard this charming forecast incessantly until I finally showed up in Budapest with a doctorate, after having spent many years in the United States. Tragically, in his eyes, his life had amounted to nothing. His last decades were dominated by flight from, or fear of, any organized authority, persisting for many years until his death, long after the war, and long after the concentration camp where he lost his wife, my mother. No amount of freedom could compensate for or relieve him of his inner demons. He was unable to acknowledge my accomplishment, as if thinking, life ain't over yet—I could still end up on the gallows.

The day after our arrival, when my three-year-old Cybèle was romping on the grass in a Budapest park, he ordered me to stop her at once.

"But Dad," I said to him patiently, "we just got here yesterday. Cybèle grew up playing on our lawn."

He thought for a while. "Never mind. If the police come, you'll get a big fine."

"That's all right—I'll pay it."

"I always knew you'd make a lousy father." With that verdict, he turned away and didn't speak to us for the rest of the day. I was back in Gallowsland.

There's yet another reason why fathers are shaming, judgmental, and mocking towards their children, and that is, "for their own good," on which we've spent a whole chapter. There are millions of fathers out there who are convinced that gentle, wise, and empathic treatment of one's child will go to their head and make them conceited. How many fathers do you know, perhaps your own, who puts his child down in front of his friends, family, or even a stranger, loud enough to make sure everyone within earshot can hear clearly? And yet in private, he sometimes sings his praises.

While in his own mind the father is convinced that anything but a putdown in front of others would go to his son's head, the real motive is likely his desire to be seen as tough, not softened by marriage and parenthood, still one of the boys. If pointed out that there are other options to deal with conceit, he would likely answer in the way my father might have, in his childrearing days: "That's for you bleeding-heart liberals who are content raising wimps and sissies who'll never amount to anything."

Then, there are fathers who do just the opposite: they demean and berate their child in private, without ever a praise, but secretly boast to others about how proud they are. Need I say, neither father is child-friendly. There was once such a man living next door, his mind made of cement. What I did, with questionable wisdom (I was much younger then), was to call to the seven-year-old girl playing in the backyard: "Mandy, sweetheart, can I have a word with you?"

"I didn't do anything." She looked and sounded terrified.

"Of course you didn't, I just want to tell you something."

Then we sat down on the lawn, separated by a wire fence. "You know, Mandy, I heard you being scolded the other day. Do you think you deserved it?"

"I don't know. I must have," she answered sheepishly. At seven, she was already brainwashed by the biggest pile of paternal crap.

"Do you really believe that?"

"My dad says so. I guess I do."

"What if I said to you that you are a terrific kid? I've known you all your life and I've never seen you do anything that wasn't terrific. Would you believe me?"

"I'm selfish, stubborn, messy, and too loud."

"Your dad is right, I'm sure—you are all those things. Did you know that all kids are like that? Kids are made to be selfish, stubborn, messy, and loud. I'd worry if you were none of those things. Would you do me one little favor? Start thinking of yourself as a kid and not like a grownup. As a child, you are right on the money."

Did I achieve anything? This single intervention, the suggestion that there was another way of looking at herself, might not have amounted to much. But it is crucial that we all become aware that with putdowns, judgments, criticism, sarcasm, mockery, and shaming we'll never raise a happy child. As adults, many of these kids will be unable to achieve a level of self-satisfaction in anything they do, and their lives will be shortchanged by lack of self-worth.

Please become aware what motivates you when you do or say something that is detrimental to your child, starting right now. It may not come easily. Our brain is a chameleon; you never know what it's thinking. To get past the camouflage requires work and painful re-examination of what you believe to be right and wrong, in order to avoid the triggers that make you utter things you really do not mean. If it's anger or frustration, try to regress into your own child's mind; remind yourself of the times when your father cut right through you with a shaming or spiteful remark. If you can feel same compassion for the child you were, you will do the same for your offspring. Nothing and I mean nothing is so important as to justify your child thinking that she should spend her life feeling ashamed of who she is.

If your attacks are rooted in disappointment, please remember that your disappointment has everything to do with your having stilted expectations in the first place. Very recently I heard a mother putting down her young daughter for chickening out at the last minute from having her ears pierced. "She's a chicken," she repeated in the store for everyone to witness. "Perhaps she just wasn't ready," I interjected.

This parent had expectations, the daughter didn't deliver, and the mother was disappointed. Rather then having empathy for her daughter, she gave in to that disappointment. What the child needed was her mother's support and permission to change her mind. Had it been a friend having her ears pierced, I am sure the mother would have said, "It's your ears, you do as you want." I happen to know that this particular parent had issues of courage all her life. Hence she expected her daughter to do better in that department than herself.

The child who becomes bound by shame has parents who should feel ashamed of themselves. I beg you not to be one of them.

CHAPTER 39

WHEN I WAS YOUR AGE

Like millions of sons before me, from the time I was about ten, I kept a mental log of the things I would never ever say to my kids. On the very top of the list I swore to myself that I would never start a conversation with, "When I was your age . . ."

What does a child hear when the father starts with "When I was your age . . ."? For starters, he will immediately shiver at the tone of delivery, making him deaf for the next five minutes. He will probably not hear anything about the hardships we endured at his age, like walking to school five miles through deep snow, or not being allowed to ever speak at the table. He will likely also miss the most educational part, about how he'd disappointed us once again, fell short of our expectations. What he may catch, sensing the end is near, is the summary: "Son, you don't know how good you have it," or "If I'd said anything like that to my father, he would have kicked my teeth in."

It's unlikely that you or anyone else could have escaped childhood without being subjected to many such reminiscences. "When I was your age" brings into focus two facts:

1. According to your father, he had a harder childhood than you did; hence whatever he dishes out you have to be grateful for.

2. There is no way you can win this contest because all the facts of the case are locked within his memory chest.

I am pretty sure that at least in the literal sense I was faithful to my resolution, never using the actual words, because had I tried, alarms would have gone off deafeningly in my head. As to the spirit of my vow, what I seem to have done was change the words enough to hide the similarity from myself. However, there was one occasion when I slipped completely. In a conversation with my son Adrian, seventeen at the time, I blurted it out, the dreaded: "When I was your age." Once uttered, of course, it's impossible to retract it.

Adrian replied without skipping a beat, as if he had been practicing for this moment for seventeen years, "Frankly, Dad, you *never*
were my age!"

First, I was stunned by his grandiose cheekiness. Then I was
hurt. I almost lashed back with a show-stopping "How dare you
speak to me like that? Who the hell do you think you are?" But a
little, wise voice pulled me back from the edge, saying, "You don't
want to go there; he's your son; not your enemy." I decided to hold
my tongue and take some time to think about what he said.

The next day when I woke up, I'd figured it out. What he meant,
quite rightly, was that to have been seventeen in the Jurassic age
of the fifties had no bearing on being seventeen in the nineties.

If I really had wanted to share with my son something about
my past, I would certainly have chosen a less confrontational
phrase. Hence, this is not an honest method of communication.
We're actually flogging our children with our experiences, rather
than conveying useful information.

We may think our experiences are similar to our children's but
they're not really similar at all. Only because we have seen the past
and we have seen the present can our brain connect the dots. If we
ask our children, the newcomers, to form a picture of our lives
twenty, thirty years ago, they could not do it. Stop for a moment
and look around the room. See how many gadgets you can pick
out. MP3, TV, CD, PC, DVD, DAT, cell phones, pagers, and God
knows what else, all of them occupying a large percentage of our
children's waking hours.

In the "old days," a child learned a good chunk of what he
knew from his parents. Today, how much has your child not learned
from you? Would you say an overwhelming amount? I know that
when some sophisticated piece of equipment turns on me, the person I call upon is my son, as a matter of course.

Our kids are smarter and know more than what we give them
credit for. On the other hand, they may be technologically more
adept, but not wiser than we were at their age. They live in a new
world and speak a new language. Therefore according to our old
standards they may appear ignorant, especially when we're cross
with them, just as they think we are ignorant. If we keep making
them feel ignorant, we will make them feel unwelcome and drive
them to spend more time with people who appreciate them more,
like their peers. And so, we dig an ever-deepening gulf between

our generations, which can only increase our state of mutual ignorance.

There are some parents we all know who, in order to bridge the gap, attempt to clone themselves into their children. They reverse the order of things—dress like their kids, adopt their lingo, want to party with them. Eventually, they're likely to discover that there is something salutary about preserving differences. When our sons, carving out their own paths, fall flat on their faces, it is comforting for them to know that it wasn't because they were like us. It is comforting for them to know that they might have fallen on their faces because they were not like us.

Our children can sense that here is something strong about the wisdom of the past, which is really a cumulative wisdom of their ancestors. When we then come to the rescue, we come well armed and in a favorable position to carry them off to safety. We could hardly do any of that if we were like them.

Although this does not mean that we have to scorn what they like and like what they scorn, even if we find that this happens in the natural course of things too frequently for our liking. From the time he was twelve, my son and I have been at odds on the subject of rap, in my opinion an obnoxious and toxic noise totally divorced from music. He would listen to it most of his waking hours. I told him he can listen to it all he wants in his own space, but that I personally don't like it and that the language is offensive to his mother and sisters.

He called me a dinosaur. Besides, he'd say, "I don't listen to the words anyway. What do you want me to listen to, opera?" "That would be nice," I said, "but for now I'd settle for you going with me to hear my favorite jazz singer of the '60s, who's coming to town." He grunted something I wasn't supposed to make out, and didn't, except I knew it was a negative, his clear answer to the invitation. As it turned out, he did come to hear Annie Ross. He couldn't have acted more bored if she had been reading the Yellow Pages. Years later, whenever I searched for one of my CDs, I was likely to find it in his room.

CHAPTER 40

THE FATHER OF THE YEAR AWARD

This was one award, my son told me years ago, that he was not going to bestow upon me.

He had wanted to go over to his friend Josh's house to hang out. I told him I had no objection, provided he completed his homework. That wouldn't do, he said, because there was a movie on TV they wanted to watch together. Couldn't he do his homework the next day, since it was Saturday? "In principle, you could," I said calmly as a veteran of many similar conversations. Experience had demonstrated that weekends were too full of activity for homework. "However, I prefer that you do the work first and hang out later. That's the order of things I want you to learn." Clearly, he and I didn't see eye to eye on the matter. My son is a pretty easygoing fellow, but schoolwork was often not his first priority, especially on weekends.

Often, when he was really committed to getting what he wanted, I conceded. But on the homework issue there was no room for argument. "I'm afraid, son," I said, "this is not up for negotiation. If you want to talk about it, I'm available, but you'll still have to do your work before you can go over to Josh's."

"That's a lousy decision, Dad," he replied, warming up. "You're a bully. What's the big deal about watching a movie first and then doing that crappy homework? I hate doing homework, anyway. It's just a huge waste of time."

"Be that as it may, the principle I'm trying to teach you is that work has to come before play."

"Yeah! Like you always do that."

"No. I don't always do it," I said, aware that I was not the symbol of virtue in that domain. "But if I had had parents who taught me that lesson at an early age, I would probably be doing much better. What I can tell you is that I always end up regretting not having done my work first. Especially after midnight when I have to struggle to stay awake to finish something I should have done days before."

"Right," he mumbled mockingly.

"Had my father taught me this lesson, he would have been unpopular at the time, but in the long run I would have been grateful and respected him for it."

Why wasn't I surprised to see his eyes rolling in their sockets, as if saying, "Oh, gag me with a spoon."

"That's just great, Dad, but can I go to Josh's, just this time?"

"No."

"Fine. I don't care about that stinking movie or about going to Josh's anyway." His voice quivering with frustration, hurt, and anger, he added, "One day I'll grow up, and I'll move far away, and you'll never see me, or maybe just once a year. And don't count on me for the Father of the Year Award."

Wow, what a crafty youngster, my son! At the age of ten he had already figured out that the threat of abandonment was a bargaining chip. Of course, he would have to hone his skills to make it into an effective chip. But where did he learn this in the first place?

After chewing on this for a few minutes, I recalled a conversation I had with my wife about my father, to which my son was witness. I was telling her how every time my father was frustrated with my sister or me, or with his lot in life, he threatened to leave us and never come back. "Of course, my sister and I were devastated," I said. "We begged him not to go. We'd do anything he wanted us to do just to stop him from leaving."

I was sure that this had been the source of my son's intelligence. Inwardly, I gave him credit for listening well and for fast thinking on his feet, but I felt uncomfortable about having planted the seed of using abandonment as a tool for eliciting concessions. Abandonment robs both parties, something of course he hadn't thought about, just like my father hadn't nearly forty years before.

"I would be very sad if you left us, Adrian," I said as he was starting his homework. "Not only would I not have the pleasure of your company, but neither would your mom and your sisters. Nor would you be able to enjoy our love. It would be terribly wasteful to punish yourself and us for not having gotten what you wanted. Perhaps you can think of some other way to tell me how upset you're with me."

"I'm not upset anymore."

"Well, the next time then. But what I came to tell you was that I'm very happy that you are my son, and also to make you a

one-time offer, take it or leave it. Okay? I'll help with your homework and then I'll drive you to Josh's."

A few years later, in a similar conversation with my daughter
Eliana, fifteen at the time, she conceded that saying no to some of
her requests worked well for her because there were times she was
secretly hoping that I'd say no.

Being temporarily unpopular is something that parents should
get used to. In fact, not being pegged to the pedestal is quite liber-
ating. Too many fathers choose never to frustrate their kids and
refuse to draw that line in the sand. The consequence? Their children don't learn how to deal with being denied anything. They
grow up to be grandiose little beings in adult bodies, feeling en-
titled to get whatever they want regardless of the cost to others.
They have a hard time with boundaries and are prone to throw
tantrums.

Did I feel bad about not having earned the coveted Father of
the Year Award? Well, yes, on the surface but no on reflection. What
I did get and continue getting from my children are their love, respect (when I behave respectably), and the pleasure of their company. But the greatest award is one I bestow upon myself, seeing
my children free from interference, striving to be competent people
in their own unique ways.

In the way of awards, I recently received a gift from Eliana, now
twenty, returning from a recent visit in Vancouver. "When I saw this,
Dad, I thought of you immediately." It was a tile with three words
on it: Live, Love, Laugh.

CHAPTER 41

WHEN YOU AND YOUR CHILD CAN'T MAKE BEAUTIFUL MUSIC TOGETHER

When my daughter Sacha was about six years old, she loved music and wanted to learn to play an instrument. For reasons that were not available then or now, she chose the violin. She was all excited about taking private lessons. Luckily, we found a wonderful teacher in our neighborhood. Her name was Jane. She had lots and lots of experience teaching young children, even though she herself wasn't yet thirty. We rented Sacha a violin appropriate in size for a six-year-old.

Since I am a major music lover as well as a frustrated musician, who excels only at playing the stereo, I was more than happy to take her and sit through her lesson while vicariously enjoying my child making her way to competence.

Things were progressing quite well. Sacha was at first a bit underwhelmed since, after several weeks of lessons and practicing, she still wasn't playing her favorite tunes. Of course, she couldn't have picked a harder instrument for short-term gratification. Yet she persevered.

To bolster her enthusiasm, I decided to also take violin lessons with Sacha. Jane saw no reason why not. In fact, she thought it was an excellent idea. We could practice together, progress, and eventually play together. "Won't it be great? We will have fun, right?" I said to my six-year-old. "Okay, Daddy, if you say so," she replied.

She couldn't have been less enthusiastic. But being a good little girl, on seeing my excitement she went along. Perhaps at six she didn't know that it was acceptable to say, "I don't want you to play violin with me. Get your own teacher, or better yet, pick some other instrument." Was she perhaps scared that I would play better, learn faster, or embarrass her with my ineptitude? Or was she looking for a way to stake her individuality and her own private domain, having four older accomplished siblings?

The long and the short of it was that practically from day one of our joint lessons my daughter became more passive, paying less attention to her teacher, and was no longer keen on practicing. I think I might have ruined it for her.

One of the factors, as I surmised afterwards, was that Sacha felt that I had horned in on her teacher, depriving her of Jane's full attention. Jane was supposed to be *her* teacher, and hence she felt betrayed by her, not only by me. Compounding this feeling, Jane had to spend a lot more time instructing me, due to my fingers' being less limber than Sacha's. Soon, practicing at home became a nuisance, with Sacha using excuses why she didn't want to practice with me. After three months of this, Jane fired us both, allegedly for health reasons.

I felt terrible for weeks, having sabotaged my daughter's musical development. But then Sacha discovered the piano and eagerly began taking piano lessons, something I too always wanted to do. Her teacher lived on our block.

Being incredibly obtuse, I asked the piano teacher if she would teach me as well. She said yes that she would, but then she forgot to show up for our first lesson. This minor slip by the teacher was enough for me to start pondering on what I was really doing. Certainly, I had violated at least two of the rules of conscious parenting, or should I say suggestions, that we should not try to be buddies to our children and thus invade their private domain, in a spirit of overzealous togetherness. Another broken rule was that I forced her to "take care of me." Sacha had said yes, when she really meant no, because she'd wanted to spare my feelings.

For the past four years, Sacha has enjoyed the piano tremendously and she plays quite proficiently. She practices even when she doesn't have to, and she is very happy when we go to hear her year-end recital. So it ended well. Which shows again that being a good-enough parent is good enough. But I will never know how Sacha would have fared with the violin.

What I did learn tonight at the dinner table, however, is another enactment of the well-known statement accredited rightly or wrongly to Sigmund Freud: sometimes a cigar is just a cigar and a cigar box is just a cigar box. Sacha, Vicki, and I were having

Sunday night dinner. Somehow the conversation turned to the drafting of this chapter. I mentioned to them that I somehow managed to misspell Sacha's name several times on the computer. She raised the question: what are you writing about me, Daddy? "About your violin lessons." "What's there to write about?" "Well," I hesitated for a moment about whether or not I wanted to go through the unpleasant experience of having to own up to her and my wife that I had screwed up by horning in on her violin lessons with Jane. I felt silly and greedy. Then I thought, I'm going for it. What's the point of writing this book if I'm not learning from it? So I told her about how I felt that I undermined her violin lessons and perhaps her lifelong enjoyment of the instrument. "I should not have started lessons with Jane, especially not right after your lessons. I ended up taking her attention away from you. I'm sorry."

Sacha looked like I was talking to her about the various techniques of counting ants in Borneo. She was definitely not going through an emotionally significant event.

"Don't worry about it, Dad," she said, more involved with her plate of raspberries than with the topic at hand. "I hated the violin. It was so hard. I sounded awful. I couldn't stand the sound of my own playing, or yours for that matter. I would have quit even if you had not been in the picture. I don't even know why I wanted to play that stupid violin; I never really liked the sound of it. I think it was mostly because I had a friend in the Suzuki class and I wanted to be with her. It had nothing to do with wanting to play the violin."

Well, so now what is the moral of the story? Not to horn in on your child's world or not to be too tempted to interpret everything according to appearances? Ultimately, whatever the reason for Sacha's abandonment of the violin, it still is a good idea to let them have some places that are just theirs without having to share with a parent. I know a ten-year-old girl who doesn't ever walk anywhere without her mom holding her hand. It is self-evident that the mother is taking her child's breath away. I see them everyday walk by my house rooting for the child to tear her hand out of the maternal grip and just run up the street all by herself all the way to the park where she'd mingle with the other children. But it never happens. Well, what I did was nowhere near so excessive, but a lesson can still be derived from it: let your child make beautiful music by herself or with one or more friends of her choosing. And if you want to play music too, go and play with the children of your own age.

And finally, based on her revelation tonight, I'm happy to have been reminded by my young daughter that often things are simpler than they seem to be. Check it out. You may save yourself some mental anguish and some emotional gymnastics.

CHAPTER 42

DON'T TEACH YOUR KID EVERYTHING YOU BELIEVE—IT MAY BE HAZARDOUS TO HIS HEALTH

Monday, July 16, in the air somewhere between West Palm Beach and Philadelphia. I'm not only up in the air; I am up in the air about an article I've just read in *USA Today*, titled "Father and Son Target Kids in Confederacy of Hate." It tells the story of a man and his pride at his young son's accomplishments: an encyclopedic knowledge of frogs and snakes, and a website the boy runs for other kids. The website is designed to promote "white supremacy and racial hate." Where did this boy acquire his inclination to disseminate bigotry and prejudice?

All fathers worthy of the name want to show the ropes to their sons and daughters. What this father illustrates is that teaching a child what he knows can be detrimental to the child. Consequently, what some fathers (and mothers) know or believe in is best kept hidden from their children. Whether or not parents can carry this off is another story. As I have touched on several times in these pages, children learn more by imitation, clues derived from offhand gestures, and facial expressions than words. So if you're not willing to question your prejudices and then flush them down the toilet, hide them under a moth-proof blanket.

Years ago, I saw a *Jerry Springer Show* episode I will never forget. The guests were young children, eight to twelve, who had learned hatred and violence from their racist fathers. These men claimed to be ordained ministers spreading the word of God. One of the children, a wholesome-looking young girl, proclaimed with fire and scorn, "God is hate, as it is written in the Bible. They are ignorant, those who believe that God is love." This child's life did not begin at the beginning, with clean white pages. This child and other children like her began life in chapter three of a hateful, cynical, and pessimistic novel. One can't but weep for children whose magic carpet was yanked from under them before they even knew of its existence.

What a contrast to Anne Frank, who in spite of pervasive evidence to the contrary, never ceased believing that people were fundamentally good. Of course, from what we know about Anne Frank, her parents were not degenerates.

Most boys will do anything to earn their fathers' love and admiration. They do it blindly and instinctively because boys (and girls, at an earlier age) are prone to regard their fathers as just this side of Superman. So if Dad is a hatemonger and openly proclaims his beliefs, the boy has little recourse but to become like Dad. Often, we can count on teen rebellion against parental values, but not with White Supremacists. Those fathers thoroughly brainwash their kids, often through their hatefully inappropriate interpretation of the Bible.

I recall a scene I once witnessed in a diner in Westchester County, New York. At the table across from me were a father and a boy, around seven. The man was visibly irritated. In a matter of ten minutes, he threw back two double scotches. "Typical woman," he complained to the boy, his voice raspy with disdain. "She said she'd be here by seven, come hell or high water. She wants to make a good impression, you see, for when she becomes your momma." At the mention of a new momma the boy started biting his nails. "Stop that! Here, have a swig—go on. Forget what they told you. I know better what's good for you."

The boy needed two trembling hands to grip the glass. He screwed up his face and downed the remains. Dad seemed content with his son's quiet obedience. Then he noticed me staring.

"What's wrong with you?" he asked, two thoughts from punching me out. "Something you wanna say?"

I recall tragically bloody memories from the 1956 Hungarian uprising against Soviet oppression. Hundreds of young children gave their lives trying to knock out Soviet tanks, armed with matches and bottles of kerosene. They learned from their elders that it was a holy cause to kill Soviet soldiers even at the risk of giving up their own lives. Many of the elders lived and died by those beliefs. And so did their kids, who had no chance to make rational and informed decisions about whether or not it was right for them to give the lives they had scarcely begun in order to earn posthumous glory.

The son in the *USA Today* article never had a chance. His father and mother kept him from outside learning by schooling him at home. The world of information available to him was through the filter of his bigoted parents. No informed teachers, kids of other persuasions, libraries, or newspapers. To date, according to the article, his website recorded over 340,000 hits, perhaps many from young visitors ravaged by racist bile.

We all have strong feelings and beliefs, some of which, alas, may not pass the test of human decency. The prejudices we acquired were not necessarily of our own making. Some we inherited from our parents and have been unable to shed, while other may have been bestowed upon us by strong proselytizers we met somewhere along the road, catching us at a vulnerable moment.

As fathers, the best way to inoculate our children against prejudice is by exposing them to ethnic diversity where we live and where they go to school. To succeed, we must make sure we live a diversified life by introducing all kinds of people into our homes. In return, we must graciously and genuinely accept invitations into the homes of their friends of other backgrounds, racial, social, and cultural. People of all races have made significant contributions. We must point these out. And when we see evidence of prejudice we must appeal to our children's sense of empathy and fair play.

To you, fathers or future fathers, who are not at all inclined to saddle society with brainwashed kids, I urge you to take protective measures immediately. Clean up your act. And do it before your child shows signs of becoming a social being.

Start a reading program. Most children take to books naturally, especially if you have been reading to them as toddlers. Pick a movie and take him to it. Talk to him age-appropriately about universal respect and diversity. Scan websites he frequents, the emails he gets from strangers. New racists no longer parade in white-hooded sheets, but they have not gone away and can be found targeting elementary school children at their most vulnerable age. Be particularly vigilant if your child is depressed. The psychiatrist Sirjay Sanger, quoted in the *USA Today* article, says, "If you have a susceptible child who is angry and depressed, the [hate] sites could push a child towards certain behavior. It's the first step towards throwing a rock." To make sure that the rock does not become a missile, find out and remedy what makes your child angry and depressed. Don't take too long to seek professional help. Be vigilant. Be wise.

Shortly after the murder of Martin Luther King Jr., there was an elementary teacher in the Midwest, so outraged by the waste of this good man that she decided to demonstrate to her class the fickleness and lack of substance of prejudice. Children with blue eyes, she told her third grade students, were smart, trustworthy, and deserving of respect. Those with brown eyes were inferior, less smart, and not deserving of privileges. The children snapped into their roles with enthusiasm, especially the blue-eyed kids. The brown-eyed kids walked around disoriented, scared, and sad, after they were shunned by their former friends, while their blue-eyed classmates quickly assumed power and enjoyed their newfound status. The next day, the teacher announced that she'd made a terrible mistake. The truly superior kids were the brown-eyed kids, and the blue-eyed kids were the inferior ones. The predictable happened. The brown-eyes kids quickly assumed power, eager to pay back for their humiliation. The third day she explained that they were all superior kids and that this had been only an experiment. (How she handled the parents' complaints was never made clear, but I have not the slightest doubt that the kids had learned a valuable lesson.)

Life is a Ferris wheel, I've been telling my children when they became old enough to grasp the substance of this story. You can be on top or on the bottom, but it doesn't change the person you are. The wheel can turn in a minute or in a year. You have to trust your own values and not be influenced by the cycles. Other people and other kids have motives of their own when they try to put you down (or build you up with flattery), but you are never privy to their inner thoughts. Conveying a sense of inner security to our children is a tough one, keeping us on our toes on a daily basis. I hardly need to point out how pivotal self-esteem is to a child's happiness and to his adult life. However, for it to be solid, the child also needs to develop a balanced regard for others. Live and let live.

CHAPTER 43

MY CHILD, MY (BELOVED) MONSTER

I want to tell you three short stories.

1. You've just spent an hour feeding your daughter, bathing, and then changing her. You want her to glow with health, well-being, and radiance. You also want to dazzle her mom. "People say fathers just ain't got it. Well, I'll show you what a dad can do!" But baby didn't land on this earth to make her father's life easier. So, just as Mom walks in the door, the baby lets go on all orifices, all within thirty seconds. "Oh, my God! What the hell did you do to my baby? I can't even go out for a few minutes!"

At such moments, your thoughts and feelings toward your baby and her mom might not be exactly overflowing with warmth.

2. You want nothing more in life than to be the most tender, the most hands-on dad in this universe and all galaxies. You've been dreaming about the wonders of being the dad to an adorable little fellow. And he is here now, just an arm's length away. You reach out for him and, to your greatest horror and shock the three-month-old tike pushes you away with both arms and looks at you with eyes that say, "Get lost, creep, or I'll call the cops. And by the way, you stink. Mommy smells delicious."

Then it happens repeatedly. In fact every time you want to pry him loose from his mom's stronghold. Now you're gradually leaning towards the theory that it's a mother-child conspiracy. You feel like running away and becoming a Big Brother to some boy who'd welcome you gratefully. What defense do you have at your disposal against the stiff-arm reflex?

3. You've been asked to come to his first grade class by Miss Emery, the teacher, who looks and sounds like she's at war with the entire world. Except, she points out that she has

grievances only against your offspring, intimating that every other parent's child is an angel. "Where does he learn such monstrous and deviant behavior? Not at school! When I ask him, he beams: 'From my dad!'" So what has he done, you wonder, inwardly glowing at your child's exemplary response. He's learning from the old man. Then she continues. "He urinates on our rubber-plant, he organizes belching and bowel gas competitions, throws sticks in the path of kids learning to ride a bicycle, he cheats at every possible game, and he licks other kids' sandwiches. Then he threatens retribution if they say a word to anyone. Oh, and just one more thing: every indication points to his failing first grade, a historic first in this school."

So suddenly, you're not so proud. You feel a failure as a father. But he couldn't have learned every one of those nasty behaviors from you, you being such an upright, well-meaning, and devoted dad. Pretty soon it sinks in.

I might as well confess. I was that father in the last example. What we considered goofing off in the home (no, we didn't have gas contests and I don't piss on the house plants) he took as acceptable behavior outside. Was he stupid? No, he was six and as yet with little sense of humor. However, he made up for it in curiosity and inventiveness. Curiosity and inventiveness, plus "if it's good enough for dad, it's good enough for me," spell mischief. After all, Dad *is* the greatest.

These three scenarios are instances of a child acting in a less than lovable manner. Your anger tells you to disown him, change his name, or yours. And yet, when your child acts the least lovable is when he needs your love the most.

Contrary to appearances, exercising the stiff-arm reflex or being told by the teacher that they are a disaster is not fun even for the moment. It shows a temporary malaise from which you can deduce that all is not well in their vision of the universe. Whether it's physical discomfort, fear, or embarrassment, the world doesn't feel a safe and hospitable place. They need to be reassured, coddled, and loved. The rule boils down to this: the worse a child behaves, the less he feels at peace. And if you reject him at those times, he will conclude that he is unlovable. The more unlovable he feels, the more he acts out and the harder you find being loving toward him.

This is not only true for a child. What do we do when we feel despondent or rejected or things don't go well at work? Are we cool, relaxed, affectionate, and generous? Or crabby, withdrawn, and punitively silent? No need to respond. We already know the answer.

What we need is counter-intuitive: a degree of generosity we have never needed to draw on before, one that allows us to put our gut on the backburner whenever our kids are in difficulty. We have much less trouble rising to the occasion when they break a bone, or a bully beats them up, or they wake up screaming from a nightmare. We identify with all of these. But when they seem to go through a discomfort, unpleasantness, or plain befuddlement, situations that we have learned to conquer in ourselves to an extent that they have become automatic and beyond our consciousness, we become much more intolerant. We have forgotten what it was like. If whatever they're going through sparks our intolerance, watch out, Junior!

Loving your child at the most challenging moments is a distillation of all that's best in you.

CHAPTER 44

MENTOR—TORMENTOR

If there were just one wish that I could be granted retroactively, it would be to have had a mentor when I was a young man. What a difference it would have made in my life, my children's and my wives'! Had I such a man to bounce my ideas off, someone who would have challenged me to explore my feelings in times when this was still unfashionable, I know I would have become a far more conscious and effective father to my children.

We'll touch on fathers and mentors several times in this book. If you have a good relationship with your father, you're lucky. Cherish it. But a father is not the best mentor for a number of very good reasons. Fathers, if they are not busy raising a second family, may be still stuck on their private agendas for their children, or sometimes even in competition with their sons. In many ways you are apt to be enmeshed in his own unfinished business.

The principal difference between a father and a mentor is that a mentor has no stake in the outcome of your decisions. Your fates are not linked. He is not offended if you do not follow his advice or proud if you do. He has no expectations of you. You cannot hurt him. You cannot toy with him. You cannot tempt him or bribe him. You cannot threaten, cajole, or otherwise manipulate him. The mentor is a magic mirror. He broadens your vision to a wider universe, allowing you to focus beyond immediate concerns and aggravations. Soon, your attitude expands. There are more dimensions to every challenge than you could ever dream of discovering on your own. The mirror lets you see the likely endpoint of diverging pathways so that you can choose knowingly. By all means, a good mentor is a good thing, and you should do what you can to find one.

The narrow-sightedness of youth is not your fault. It is the way we are built. When I was eighteen, I saved up a huge amount of money to buy a 35mm camera, an Edixa SLR, the only half-decent camera I could afford, with interchangeable lenses. I didn't have the money to buy additional lenses, but even so, for a while I felt on top of the world. But soon I desperately craved a telephoto lens. I saved up another pile of money to buy a 135mm lens, and then a 200mm lens, and finally a 300mm lens that was so big and clumsy I had to take along a friend on shoots. Eventually, after I had everything I thought I wanted, taking pictures became too much of a chore.

By chance, I met an amateur photographer named Nicola, who was about fifty, one of the judges in a contest I entered.

"Why this obsession," he asked me after the show, "with taking something small and far away and blowing it up out of proportion?" I was stunned by his heresy. All I could say after a while was that's what telephoto lenses were designed for. "Precisely," he replied, "which is why great photographers almost never use them."

Then he said that I had potential and he would be willing to review my work and oversee my progress. I never took him up on it, considering him with my youthful arrogance an old fuddy-duddy.

Over the next few years I discovered that most beginners gravitate to long lenses. It is less complicated to pick out a face without the background throwing off composition, a single rock instead of a rock garden, a tree instead of a forest. It is much more difficult to take in the total picture than focus on one little element. Nicola was talking about life, not photography. I never met him again but I thought much later that he was my mentor who arrived too soon, one I let slip between my fingers.

The sad fact of life is that while we're young we're convinced that we are the ultimate experts in what is good for us. And because of a thick armor of certainty, it is almost impossible to convince us otherwise. Our door is closed to differing points of view. Such is the arrogance of youth. Unless some trauma befalls us that force us to re-examine our lives in a totally different light, we'll just have to sit back and await the softening effect of maturity. Only then do we discover that many beliefs we held as the sacred truth are neither sacred nor true.

A mentor coming at just the right time can help us dismount from our high-horse and help us see that we are not a finished product even if we are state-of-the-art at any given time; that we still have some growing up to do and much to learn from tomorrow. The question then remains: how do we find a mentor?

A mentor will not come after you. He may make a gesture of availability but it will be up to you to nail him down. Those of us who trust in serendipity or cosmic forces may want to believe that he will likely be there when the time is right. For the rest of us we have to work to find him.

Make yourself available. Be in places where you can find men of different ages—hobby groups, cycling groups, church groups. Keep your eyes and ears open for a conversation that has to do with feelings. You won't find him dwelling on numbers—like football or hockey scores, or horsepower, speed or distance, the Dow Jones averages, or the size of a woman's breasts. You won't find him grandstanding on politics, scheming to make money, or engaging in idle gossip. A mentor has no need to be heard and therefore does not need to raise his voice. You can tell by the aura of loudness in a person that you are on the wrong track. Keep in mind that a mentor doesn't have to have a doctorate in philosophy. He doesn't even have to have his own life in impeccable order, provided he lives in a way that is not destructive to himself or others. But he must have an interest, ability, and willingness to listen to *you*.

He may be the crusty supervisor or a foreman at work. Or the old Sicilian barber, who has been cutting your hair for years, or a former high school teacher, hockey coach, or bandleader. Or for that matter, someone who has been taking the same bus to work, with whom you happened to strike up a conversation about nothing.

How do you know he is the right man for the job? For openers, you suddenly find yourself telling him things you never thought you would divulge to anyone, and to your surprise you are doing it in comfort and without embarrassment. As you get to know him more, you may find you don't know a hell of a lot about him because he doesn't push his history on you. He speaks of himself only when you invite him to do so.

A word of caution: Just as there are false prophets, you can find false mentors who can lead you astray. Don't confuse a peaceful face and voice with the expressionless drone of men who are absent from their own lives, let alone someone else's. If he asks, "Well, did you do what I told you?" he is a false mentor. The real mentor seldom uses "I."

CHAPTER 45

THE NAKED TRUTH

A young client called me frantically one Monday morning.

"Dr. Stein, I have to come and see you right away."

"I'm fully booked, Brendan," I said, "but can we talk on the phone at lunchtime?"

"No, not on the phone. God, I'm really scared."

I knew Brendan to be a level-headed guy. This must have been a real emergency. "Okay, come at six-thirty." I already had a five-thirty add-on, so I was not overly pleased. It's hard to find the right balance between devotion to family and duty to clients.

As my five-thirty was leaving, Brendan was pacing in front of the door.

"I didn't go to work," he said, "and I couldn't stay at home—I just couldn't bear to be with them. So I spent the day walking on the Lakeshore, and then I walked here."

"You do look a bit disheveled," I said generously, for he looked a whole lot worse than that.

I have been seeing Brendan weekly for a few months, now. What had brought him to me were problems at work. His bosses, in a rapidly expanding software business, insisted on promoting him to higher and higher positions, with more and more people reporting to him. With each promotion, he felt incapable of assuming added responsibility, yet his performance proved otherwise. But this seemed different. "I take it this is not about work," I said.

"I wish it was," he said. "This is much, much worse than another promotion."

I smiled and kept quiet. That he maintained a sense of humor in his state of agitation was a good sign. It was as if a deeper part of Brendan knew that things were not as bad as they seemed, and I was fairly confident that he would be going home that night much relieved. It also helped that Brendan belonged to a very select group of my clients who had a picture book marriage, with a supportive and adoring wife and a pig-tailed daughter of just over three.

"Last night, Veronica and I went to bed around eleven. We were making love for about ten minutes or so when Kit woke up and started crying. She just woke up; we didn't wake her. So I said to Veronica, I'll take care of it. I put on my pajama bottoms and went to Kit's room. She'd had a nightmare and I could see right away that this wasn't going to be one of those kiss-kiss-and-goodnight events. So I picked her up and we went to the kitchen for a glass of apple juice. That didn't do the trick, so I took her to the living room and we sat in front of the TV set, ready to watch *A Bug's Life* if it became absolutely necessary, for the hundredth time."

"Go on."

"I'm rambling. Anyway, Kit was trying to tell me her nightmare and I just couldn't get it. You know how three-year-olds talk. So I played along as best as I could until finally she settled down somewhat, but not enough to consider going back to bed. Okay, I said, five minutes, young lady, not one minute more, and turned on the video."

Now, Brendan was becoming tearful and I began to have an inkling of where this might be going. "Please continue," I prompted.

"I was starting to doze off, with Kit squirming and wiggling in my lap. But just before nodding off completely, I suddenly realized that I was getting an erection. Can you imagine? A father getting an erection from his three-year-old? I feel like a total degenerate. I ask you, what sort of a man does that?"

Brendan was sobbing, loud, and unrestrained. I handed him a box of tissues and pulled up closer to him. I felt a deep compassion for this young man whom I knew to be well intentioned and trying very hard to be a good father. Also, I was remembering some of the ridiculous times that I had struggled with unwanted erections.

When he had composed himself, I asked what happened next.

"Well, the first thing I did was cross my legs and shift Kit away from the offending member. Thank God, she didn't ask what it was, poking her. Then I carried her to bed, this time without protest. Then I sat out on the balcony shivering, only partly from the cold, and tried to figure it all out. I looked at it this way and that, but the conclusion always came out the same: I was dirty and disgusting and I would have to take myself away from my family."

"Do you feel better now that you told me?"

"You haven't thrown me out . . . yet. That counts for something."

"Now think about this carefully before you answer: do you have any sexual feelings toward your daughter?"

"No, I swear! On my mother's life."

"Do you have sexual feelings toward other children?"

"No!"

Let's leave Brendan for a moment. Think back. What were the circumstances of your single most inappropriate erection?

Adolescent men often walk around with their dicks doing the royal salute. Crowded buses, streetcars, the dance floor are minefields threatening to blow up under their feet. The best self-defense in these loaded situations is concealment: hide the damn thing out of sight before they get accused of perversion. From what my young adult son and his friends tell me, today is a completely new ball game. Many twenty- or thirty-something men (and women) are much more relaxed about their sexuality and its manifestations. "Ultimately it's not a bigger deal for a girl to notice an erect dick than for her to go around topless and in an ass-floss thong," said Jane, a young woman client, speaking about an experience she'd had with her boyfriend on a Caribbean beach.

Around puberty we are all walking erections. I remember, as a teenager, riding the bus several stops past my destination because I couldn't get up from my seat. I got into the habit of carrying a jacket draped over my arm, which did a reasonable job of concealment but also made me a bit eccentric in the hot days of summer. Even in my twenties, when going on dates, I could not relax and enjoy myself because I was constantly adjusting my position with respect to my date's point of view. And dancing? Forget it. Of course in those days we didn't get laid much, if at all. In today's environment, I would just as likely comment to my date, "Honey, this thing is bothering me. Would you please do something about it?"

When I saw Brendan on his regular appointment later that week, he was completely relieved about the incident and was starting to ponder what his difficulties at work and his shame at home had in common, which put him on the fast track for improvement.

Why are men so afraid of their erections? Why do they immediately assume the worst? Most young men are shy about their penises, particularly in front of females, regardless of age. They've been taught to think of the penis as a dangerous instrument only to be unsheathed with a consenting partner. Often, what I find is that young fathers like Brendan are fearful that they may be lapsing into perverted fantasies and even actions towards their kids. Why? Because it's the lascivious way men are built, according to the rumor mill.

In a similar vein, men find themselves awkward with their young children, afraid of their strength, their lack of finesse. They fear that they might drop them or otherwise hurt them through clumsiness. It takes apprenticeship and often an assertive and encouraging partner to convince them that they can be trusted with their babies. Underneath the gruff exterior, most men are born daddies.

Adding to the natural shyness of men about their sexuality is the prevailing attitude of political correctness, obsessed with finding instances of abuse wherever men are in contact with kids, especially girls. And because men tend to be shy and fearful in the company of younger children, they sit as natural targets, finding it difficult to mount an impromptu defense.

Political correctness, coming on the heels of the feminist movement, has made the eunuch the poster boy of a safe male. Any departure from this model risks the censure of the self-appointed Committee on Hard-Ons, because as everyone knows, a naked man is a dangerous man, and a man with an erection is a potential rapist. A lot of us seem to have assimilated political correctness unquestioningly and have become terrified at our own healthy sexuality.

Healthy men, especially young men, have erections for no reason. Anything brushing against our penis, a full bladder, the sun warming our crotch, a poodle on our lap, an errant thought of which we're even unaware, can pump up the rod. This does not turn us into monsters or make us lose control.

So, Brendan, to your agonizing self-reproach: "What sort of a man would do that?" The answer is Everyman.

A discussion about sexual matter in the home would not be complete without looking at boundaries: what is safe and unsafe, and what is appropriate. Appropriate turns out to be quite elastic and culture-dependent, but even so there are boundaries.

The most frequent concern young fathers grapple with is how much nudity and at what age? Can I take a shower or a bath with my young child? Is it okay for me to sleep in the nude and welcome her into our bed? Can we change clothes in front of the child without arousing or encouraging their sexual curiosity? What if we were to take the child to a beach where nudity is lawful?

Children at a very young age notice that the opposite-sex parent looks different from them "down there." When they become old enough to ask or comment about this difference, they make innocent inquiries about it. If you're comfortable with your own nude body, you'll be able to respond matter of factly, acknowledging the difference. If, however, you're more reserved or uptight about it, you'll avoid being seen naked by your child. These fathers may be awkward and harbor misgivings about seeing their bodies or their toddlers' naked, let alone touch them when they're bathing, drying, or towelling their private parts.

Keep in mind that, at a tender age, your child has no notion about how one part of the body differs from another. So, if you naturally tend to her (or his) body parts without lingering over or probing or making funny remarks about private parts you will be sending a message that everything is fine with his body and he would have no reason to become more curious about his penis than his elbow. Later, when you're likely to be sharing a bath or a shower, or changing side by side in a locker room, treating these activities as a "bath," "a shower," or "changing clothes," there will be nothing to communicate to your child that it is more than just what it seems to be. It is your level of spontaneity or lack of it that will determine whether you define the occasion as routine or as sexual. Children are always looking for clues as to how to attach values to all facets of human behavior. By absorbing ours they learn to find their place in the world. They are exceedingly sensitive to nuances of speech, facial expression, or gesture. Two hours of indoctrination are nothing compared to the instantaneous and often unconscious expressions that define our own attitudes and prejudices. It hardly helps to expound on poverty and how an unfortunate beggar came to be a beggar when you have already betrayed your own attitude of revulsion.

When you notice your son blatantly looking at your or other people's genitals in a locker room, your best bet is still to make no comment until he initiates a dialogue. "Daddy, your penis is much smaller then the man next to you."

Try not to swallow your tongue or express shock. You could say for instance, "You're right sweetheart, it is smaller. Some men's are smaller than others."

"Why, Daddy?"

"We're just made that way. Just like cows have horns and horses don't."

"Daddy, my penis stands up in the bathtub, and it gets really small in the swimming pool."

"Yes, Justin, that's how we are built." And then proceed as if this were a routine, everyday conversation. When you come home, burning to share this dialogue with your spouse, do it privately; otherwise, the mere repetition will engrave the incident into the child's budding value map.

My general rule of thumb around these matters is to track the child. When he indicates an interest, I'll reply age-appropriately without offering too many details for which the child is neither ready nor asking for. The same goes for being nude in front of him. When my children began to stop changing in front of me or shut the bathroom door, I did the same.

One of my clients was going to Europe with his seven-year-old daughter for a summer vacation. Their itinerary included some of the Mediterranean beaches where nudity is routine. "What do I do? Should we skip those beaches or should we risk taking our daughter?"

I answered, "If the two of you have been relaxed with your daughter about nudity at home, I'd take her to the beach and from the corner of my eye check out her reaction to the scene. If she acted cool, so would I. If, on the other hand, your child has never seen you naked, I would not initiate her to nudity in public."

A day will come when your kid's natural innocence will give way to modesty. That's the time to pack it away. When he or she no longer asks for a back or tushy rub, you'll know that your child has entered the world of sexual awareness. It will last a lifetime. But let no one tell you that because your daughter has breasts, you can no longer hug her. And do continue to hug your son. A lot of men never had hugs from their dads and are now in psychotherapy working on emotional desolateness. As the cliché goes, sometimes a cigar's just a cigar.

CHAPTER 46

GOODBYES

1.

A great challenge for a father is helping his young child through the dark corridors of losing a beloved grandparent. In addition to being unable to find anything useful in our bag of wisdom, we also find ourselves depleted or even debilitated by our own grief. It seems we cannot go on—and then we do. Our child needs us more than ever before. She needs to know with a visceral sense that even though Grandma as she has always known her is gone from her life, the family continues to thrive and the child's world, although diminished by the loss, continues on a safe journey.

I'm writing these words on our return flight between Palm Beach and Charlotte, North Carolina, around 7:30 a.m. on a sunny June day. Sacha, my youngest, is in the seat next to me, more asleep than awake. Eliana, nineteen, is one seat away, and Adrian, an adult but in many ways a child, behind me, hiding under his headset, comatose. My wife, Vicki, has stayed behind, to share a few more hours with her mom. Hilda's spirit has already loosened its strong-hold on her body. It is ready to go wherever spirits go. Her oxygen-deprived brain had already begun its migration of its own, that can no longer be accessed by her loved ones.

We've known for a while that my mother-in-law was not much longer for this world. She had struggled for a long time, and she kept winning her fights against one disease after another. Yet we were not acutely aware of the toll this was taking on her body. And so, we were not as diligent in preparing Sacha for the last decline as we should have been.

Ten days ago we got the call: Mom's cancer had returned, and it was all over her body. There was no time to waste; we had to hurry to say goodbye.

My wife and I told Sacha in a voice muffled more by sadness, fear, and grief than tranquility that this time Grandma would not be getting better. "She is not suffering," I added, "and she is not going to suffer. One day or night, soon, perhaps very soon, she will close her eyes and her spirit will leave her body. It is her body that the cancer has invaded, not her spirit. Her spirit is healthy and robust and it needs to soar. The grandma you have always known and loved has already left. What is still there is just a shadow of Grandma, weak and sick. Her body can no longer carry on."

"As soon as she can get a flight, Sachi," I continued, "Mommy will take a plane to be with Grandma. They need to be alone to say goodbye to each other. Then, I'll take you, Eliana, and Adrian to see her and to tell her how much we've loved her and will continue to love her forever. And we'll wish her strength and courage for the journey ahead."

I felt my blood turning to ashes in my veins, as I had just evicted this young child from the tangible innocence of life, a life she'd considered everlasting. At first, my words seemed to make no impact. She said nothing, looked nowhere.

That night, we improvised a bed on the floor in our bedroom. Vicki and I listened to Sacha tossing and turning, unable to surrender to sleep. To be sure, we were no better, consumed by our anguish about what was waiting for our entire family and not the least for Hilda, the mother and grandmother we all loved and respected.

Eleven o'clock, way past Sacha's bedtime on a school night. She is still restless. I straighten her blanket when I notice her back rhythmically heaving. She is silently sobbing as if not wanting to disturb us with her pain. After all, what could we or anybody do? Many children are very private with their vulnerabilities and their grief, as if ashamed of their pain.

I squatted next to her and began gently stroking her back, like when she was really little and couldn't fall asleep. She is tall and strong for her age, yet once again she feels so small. The infinitely small pitted against the forces of the infinitely great.

"Sacha, Sachi, Sachenka," I whisper in her ear the chant I had woven of all her names years ago when she used to lie against my chest rocking us both to sleep. "You're not alone, Mommy is here, your brother and sisters are here, and I'm here. We're all together facing this. Grandma is not leaving us; she is leaving her body riddled with cancer. You'll be able to see her, talk to her, and she'll talk back to you as she has always done. But instead of seeing her with eyes that look outside, and listening to her with your ears that hear the noises of the world, you'll discover that your eyes and ears sense only what's inside you."

I knew she heard me. But to respond was beyond her emotional means. I more or less expected that. Children process their grief internally.

"We must let her go, Sachi, so that she can free herself of her sick body." I felt her body convulse against the palm of my hand, and soon she let out the howl of a wounded animal. Eventually, after an hour or two, Sacha anguished herself to sleep.

Vicki and I held on to each other the whole night. My thoughts were racing, the same thought over and over, like a dog chasing its tail. I realized I was not able to do what I suggested my child should do. None of us were willing or able to let the dying woman go. Yet we the parents had to pretend otherwise, because if Sacha had seen the depth of our sorrow, she would have fallen deeper into her own, without the safety net of our bringing her out. And so it is; in the process of trying to heal our children we also heal ourselves, for they link us to life and the succession of generations.

Since we were unable to get a flight for several days, we had a chance for a few more conversations with Sacha. One night, she cuddled up to us in bed and said in a baby voice: "I'm sad about grandma."

"So are we, sweetheart," we both said in reply.

"Yeah, but you got to spend a long time with her. I knew her for such a short time. It's not fair."

"You're right, Sachi, it's a rip-off." I supported her indignation, together with her impeccable logic.

Another evening, Vicki had late clients so I was the parent in charge. I cooked Sacha's favorite dinner. My colleague and bereavement specialist, Dr. Ed Pakes, had told me a long time ago to feed the bereaved with whatever feels like chicken soup. In Sacha's case it was spaghetti with my homemade Bolognese sauce.

Before bed, she brought up Grandma again, letting me know that she needed to talk and that she needed comforting.

"Sachi, my love," I said, "you'll probably be sad for quite a while and Grandma is not even dead yet." (I made a mental note that this was the first time that I could say the word without it sticking in my throat.) "The grandma who used to take you to the playground, play games with you, tell you stories, bring you gifts, stayed with you when Mommy and I went on a trip has already left this life. But when she breathes her last breath, her spirit—that thing which makes us who we are—will rise from her body and seek another body to dwell in. Just like when you were growing in your mommy's tummy, your spirit was out there in the universe looking for a new body. And your spirit chose you as her next life. And that's how you became you. Your spirit looked down into our world and said, 'Now that's a nice and friendly family, I can see myself going there. I know they'll love me.' And so you came. You chose us."

"So perhaps in another life I was a dolphin," said Sacha, trying very hard to make sense of what I said. She seemed to be speaking more to herself than to me. I also noticed that for the first time in days, she had an energized lilt to her voice. "Perhaps that's why I love dolphins so much." Then, hesitantly, she asked, "Daddy, when a dolphin dies, what happens to the little dolphins?"

Death of a parent is the darkest and deepest chasm in a child's imagination. If contemplated at all, it is too foreboding to dwell on for more than a millisecond. "Well," I said, "that happens very rarely."

She thought some more. "What if the mother gets killed by a boat?"

"If that happens, the other dolphins rush in to take care of the young ones."

"Okay," she said, seemingly satisfied, perhaps not wanting to remove the veneer of safety from our conversation.

Was I telling the truth or was I just managing her? Would I have agreed to just about anything to make it easier for her to cope? Do I believe in the eternal life of spirits, where they come from, and where they go when they leave the inert body? I honestly don't know. I just hope that our spirits go to peaceful places, and perhaps even that when we die we reconnect in some way with the spirits of those who had left us behind. I hope that in some way my spirit will always be in touch with my children's spirits, for losing them forever is a very sad and scary thought, the equivalent of the child's contemplation of the loss of a parent. All this, however, was too much to tell to a distraught young child.

"There are people who have the special gift of getting in touch with the spirits of people we used to know. They're called channellers."

"You mean they could help me speak to Grandma when she arrives in her new place?" said Sacha, her face lighting up.

"Yes, very likely." Strange as it may sound, this time I was telling the truth. In the height of my skepticism about channellers, many years ago, I had the extraordinary experience of sitting beside an elderly lady on a flight to Florida. After half an hour of casual conversation, she made the suggestion of getting me in touch with the spirit of my mother. I hadn't said a word about my mother to that point. To my greatest and most humbling surprise, she put her hand on mine and indeed connected me to my mother whose voice I heard coming from her throat and whose warmth I felt on my hand. So, I had no qualms reassuring Sacha that it was entirely possible to connect one day with her grandma's spirit.

After our conversation, she seemed to be more at peace. A few minutes before our trip she asked, "Daddy, is Grandma going to get better?"

"No, Sachi, she is too sick to get better."

"I know," she answered in a quiet voice.

2.

Hilda's husband had died fourteen years before. Our son, Adrian, was ten and Eliana seven, Sacha not yet born. A phone call informed us of my children's beloved Grandfather Aaron's sudden death. The relationship between those two kids and their grandfather was nothing short of magical, although he lived in Florida and they in Toronto. Meeting only a few times a year, their bond proved that quality supersedes frequency.

As is characteristic of boys, Adrian buried his pain and bewilderment deep inside a well of silence. To this day, he will talk to us about anything but the experience of losing his grandfather. To me, it had seemed like he felt expelled from paradise. Eliana appeared confused about the whole thing. She had always been a very happy child, contented with almost everything. She had little familiarity with loss and grief. At seven, children who grow up in harmonious surroundings can't even conceptualize what could possibly strike the sun from their sky. Death doesn't come close to figuring on the horizon.

On receiving the news, we had told the children that we had to catch the first available flight to attend Poppa's funeral and the Shiva—the Jewish version of a wake. The last time Eliana and Adrian had seen their grandfather, he was alive and as vigorous as always.

"What's a funeral, Daddy?" my seven-year-old asked.

"It's a chance for all of us to say goodbye to Poppa," I replied.
"That's silly, Daddy," she said indignantly. "We should have said goodbye when he was still alive."

Those were the only words she ever spoke about her grandfather's death. But, without a doubt, for quite a while, both my children had lost their boundless exuberance.

When we arrived in Florida, Aaron's extended family decided that the younger children should not attend the funeral. I disagreed but not forcefully enough. I still fret about my priorities then—drawing back, rather than adding to the family's upset. There are times when children need us to be wise, courageous, and empathic to their needs, to the exclusion of adult convenience and sensibilities. That had been one of those times, a time when I fell short of insisting on my own convictions.

Because the news had hit them unprepared, they were robbed of the opportunity to say farewell to their grandfather, to tell him how much they loved him and how much fun they had had with him. Because they were denied participating in his departure, his death never became concrete to them. One clear day, they were told that their grandfather had passed away and that they would never see him again. Children are concrete beings; they think in terms of their senses, what they see and hear. Even with death, they cope better when given a chance to witness the facts. (I don't mean that they should witness the throes of a person dying.) They need to go to the funeral, see exactly what is happening, and be part of the final send off. The ritual and the communal tears make sense to them. It is also crucial for them to learn that even though someone everyone loved has left the fold, the rest of the family continues as a solid unit.

I have good reason to believe that my son, who adored his grandfather, still hasn't made closure fourteen years later. As for Vicki and me, we resolved that we would never make the same mistake again.

As I write these words, I'm reminded of my late sister's words. She had been fighting against a killer cancer when somebody said to her in what was supposed to be an optimistic vein: "You have to go on, you know. Hope is always the last to die." And my terminally ill sister Agi replied: "Actually no. Hope never dies."

CHAPTER 47

THE THOUGHT OF LOSING YOUR CHILD

Anybody who has reached the age of adulthood has had at least one close experience with death. It is therefore only natural that as a father, one day, you'll be seized by a sudden panic: "Oh my God! What if she died," thinking of the one thing that you couldn't face losing, the unimaginable catastrophe. The sixteenth-century French philosopher Michel de Montaigne proclaimed that he didn't allow himself to feel attached to his children because they "tend to die very young."

Although these days children in our parts of the world seldom die because of poor sanitary conditions, medical ignorance, epidemics, or starvation, that hardly protects us from the nightmarish fantasy. And if you ever had a child die, the overwhelming fear of losing a second child may never leave your side for as long as you live.

For some reason, even without a past history of a close relative's untimely demise, some people become so morbidly obsessed with the specter of death that they weave a cocoon around their children. This makes the children look and act differently from others, as if they lived in a state of emotional and physical incarceration, which they do. All I can say is if you're one of these people, seek professional help. And if you're married to one of these people, seek professional help.

"If anything happened to my little guy," a new father told me recently, "I would simply die. There's no way I could survive." Another man in my men's group, about fifty years old, told the group he would rather "cop out of the whole enterprise than to expose myself to the possibility of my kid dying before me." Which is why he never fathered a child, although he has been in a solid marriage for over twenty years.

There's no way I'm going to take a cavalier approach to this topic. I have lived through life-threatening crises with three of my five children. When my first-born was ten days old, for nearly two days we didn't know if she would live or not. My son, through youthful excesses and carelessness, has already stared death in the eye twice in his young life. My youngest, Sacha, ingested some toxic substance at eighteen months. Needless to say, on each occasion, I as a parent felt as close to death's door as my child. Today, years later, with all my children healthy and thriving, I still shudder at the memory. Losing a child is the worst thing that can happen to you. It changes your life forever. The parents I know who have suffered this loss have never really recovered completely, ten, twenty, or thirty years after the fact.

Having said that, need I remind you that everything in life is a gamble and that the greater the gain, the bigger the risk? Of course, everybody has a personal comfort level with the amount of risk he can digest. I certainly don't pull out my calculator before boarding a Boeing 747, but somewhere inside some remote convolution in my brain, somebody *is* calculating and reasoning and coming to some conclusion. "Oh well, we're facing a situation here of certain death but the chances are .001% and there's that nude beach in Martinique, so I guess we can put up with the odds for now."

There's a completely different category of men who don't want children because "this is too imperfect a world to impose a life sentence on yet another innocent child." I have an easier time countering this argument, founded on an overdeveloped sense of idealism. People in this idealistic camp live in a perpetual state of disappointment as they drag themselves through existence, feeling betrayed because nothing measures up to their unrealistic projection of what life should be like. The false tenet here is that they believe people have children for children's sake. Far from it. In this world, people have children for their own (hopefully healthy) selfish reasons.

Successfully countering an argument and changing people's minds are two different propositions. After all, these parents have made a career of avoiding the responsibility of parenthood. That is, until by some accident, one of these men should become a father. Well, you've never seen a more magical transformation. Within weeks there is a totally new philosophy to replace the old, and the baby is the best thing that ever happened to them. Unfortunately, too often they tend to relapse in adversity, for a shorter or a longer time depending on the degree of adversity. On the whole, I have come to believe that people whose life philosophy hinges on an unrealistic image of the world probably shouldn't have children. There's too much at stake.

A psychiatrist colleague of mine, who has worked for years in a hospital for children with incurable illness, told me the poignant story of a child of nine years of age. The child, a beautiful, hazel-eyed girl with blonde hair, had made peace with herself about her impending passing but was forced into a superhuman effort to stay alive as long as possible in spite of a great deal of pain every minute of every day and night. Why? "Because my parents said if I died, so would they."

A child should not be burdened with the safekeeping of her parents' lives. "When I hear you talking about not being able to go on living if you lost your son," I said to my young client, "this sounds as if you had made your son responsible for your life." This was not a glib assertion. There are lots of parentified children pressed into the duty of looking after their parents, at a very young age. This unnatural reversal of roles bears bitter fruit. A child needs parents to give him the security to blossom, to experiment, to grow, to experience the whole gamut of life. A parentified child is just as much in a cocoon as the overprotected child. Both these extremes of parent-child relationships are prevalent in Holocaust survivor families and their children's families, for understandable reasons.

I knew a woman who at the age of sixteen was sexually abused by a Nazi hoodlum. Shortly after this, her parents were killed. Somehow, years later, she was able to put her life back together, endowed with tremendous inborn resilience, and with the help of a capable therapist. Later, her young son died of a brain tumor. How does a person like this survive? Not only did she survive but she ended up raising vast amounts of money for cancer research, and she formed a chapter of the Bereaved Parents of Ontario. There isn't a day she doesn't think of her son, but her life continues with sufficient value for her to go on, while living a productive life.

Why am I writing about the death of a child in this upbeat, optimistic book for new fathers, creators of life? Just like every person who's ever had a drink is a potential alcoholic, an encounter with death of someone close to you can consume you over time until you become a living corpse. We must convince ourselves that the death experience we lived through was not a universal experience, transferable to another person you loved. It is a mistake to infect our children with our fears.

CHAPTER 48

ALL YOU NEED IS LOVE

After nearly twenty years of working as a psychotherapist, I've come to a few conclusions. I may not have set the horizon ablaze with my ground level enlightenments, and it's entirely possible, even likely, that others have come to the same conclusions before me. Nevertheless, I consider them highly important because I organize my life—as do you—according to private discoveries. I've been offered many pieces of wisdom that could have worked for me had I discovered them myself. It is a fundamental principle of psychotherapy not to tell the client what he or she should do or even what would be wise for him or her to do. The therapist who does that robs the client of the fruits of discovery so essential to our personal growth.

I can hear some of you say, "This makes little sense from the pen of a man offering young fathers instances of wisdom. What about *our* need to discover on our own what works and what doesn't?"

I'm in full support of you following your own path. What I mean is that while no one can discover the world on his own, we all need the guidance of what has been learned before us by others. Rather than following the whole knowledge ball of anyone else, I'm happy to take bits and pieces from whatever source. At the same time, I reject the thoughts, beliefs, and practices that I deem counterproductive to living my life mindfully and responsibly. At the end of the day, however, I'll end up with my unique shake of the kaleidoscope. And tomorrow and all subsequent days it will be the same process. This is what I'm promoting to fathers in this book and everywhere else.

Having said this, one of the conclusions that I want to address is here is about the relationship between how we view ourselves and how we operate as fathers. The process unfolds like this. Based on one or several details of our early history, we come to formulate some mistaken beliefs about ourselves as men, and consequently, as fathers. Drawing on these beliefs we come to bad decisions about the way to conduct our lives. These bad decisions then result in destructive or counterproductive actions. When confronted with the consequence(s) of these actions, we end up feeling bad about ourselves and, naturally, we formulate brand-new mistaken beliefs about the kind of fathers we are going to be or that we already are and will always be. And there we go, one more time around this downward spiral. The result for many men is that they never end up being the fathers they'd like to be and that their children don't have the fathers they need, crave, and deserve.

Here is a story to illustrate what I mean.

Walter is the youngest of three sons born to an upper-crust couple of Dutch extraction. Without any doubt, according to the autobiography he drafted as part of his therapy, mother was the power broker in their mansion in Rosedale, a patrician section of Toronto. Father took care of business, mother took care of everything else, including father and their children. The stern matriarch was generous with her unsolicited insights about everything from the infinitely small to the infinitely large. They all knew that her truths were unimpeachable. It is in that spirit that she handed down her rules of conduct and her opinion about everything and everybody.

On top of her list of rules was that her children were never to utter a word of complaint or raise their voices in self-defense. If need be they will offer their lives for their way of life, the lofty ideals of their peers, and the Queen, but they were never to pronounce a word to assert themselves. As for Walter, she made no secret of her assessment. Her two older sons were brilliant from their early childhood on and they never disappointed her, but her youngest was a constant source of resignation and frustration. "Peter and John are well suited to enter the family business and make brilliant contributions to it, but my poor-poor Walter will never amount to anything. He has been dull and lackluster from the first day of his life and I see no hope that there will be any change in the unfortunate boy's future. He will always be a burden on the family."

Walter has always thought of himself as a brooding child and adolescent, with a slow wit and borderline performance in all that he had undertaken.

Based on what he always thought of as a biographical curse, Walter formulated the mistaken belief that he was worthless with nothing to offer to anyone, including a potential wife. As such, he believed that becoming a father one day would be out of the question. He would be nothing but a handicap to a child.

At nineteen, after just barely finishing high school, Walter decided that it was time for him to disappear from this family where he believed he clearly didn't belong. So, with a little inheritance he got from an uncle, he was off to Europe.

London, Amsterdam, Paris. Wherever he went, he got into one untoward encounter after another. Most of the time, it had to do with bad decisions centering around his mistaken beliefs about himself: "If I'm a worthless piece of shit, I may as well live a worthless life." That kind of thinking led to sizable gambling debts, street and barroom fights, issuing bad checks.

Amid all the chaos of his vagabond life, he met Chrissy, a young English woman with a biographical baggage that seemed like the carbon copy of Walter's own. They kept company for three months when the two twenty-year-olds learned from her doctor that she was pregnant. Chrissy saw in the news a blessed message about the wisdom of settling down. Walter, her brooding and silent partner, as usual had little to say for or against keeping the child. He went along, it would seem, out of inertia with everything Chrissy wanted. He had been used to having a woman telling him what to do or not do. As always, he didn't think that disagreeing or even discussing it was even an option.

So Chrissy wanted to get married in England and then move to Toronto. That's what they did. He got a meaningless job in the family's business to earn enough to support his wife and child modestly. Without even realizing the passage of time, Walter lived sunken into himself. His work demanded little of him. So he spent his down time playing solitaire or other computer games. And he drank quietly but surely, to numb the time that caused him pain, as he had said it once in his therapy session. He did such a good job that he was oblivious to the fact that while in Toronto, in rapid succession, the couple had three more children. Since he had chosen to exclude himself from his own life, naturally, he didn't emerge much to his children either. "I wanted to protect them from me," he declared. "I was bad news. Not only had they no need for me, they needed to be away from me."

As the children were growing up, Walter rejected all of them, one by one, except the youngest, Wendy. She became the chosen child whose mandate was to make it all good for her father. That was too heavy a burden for the young woman. She consequently concluded, as her father had done many years before, that she was no good. So it was now her turn to make bad decisions about conducting her life. She was mindless of her health, finances, relationships. All those bad decisions led to self-destructive actions that eventually put her life in crisis: she ended up teetering between life and death as the outcome of a crack cocaine binge. She hung to life on a thread. The doctors and medical technology saved her from premature death, but her spirit was severely damaged.

Almost losing his daughter to cocaine shook up Walter enough that he chose to go into psychotherapy. We're in the process of re-examining his beliefs about himself and what he needs to change in his actions that are a direct outcome of his disastrous core beliefs about himself.

This story is just one of the countless ways to illustrate the chain that links bad news from childhood to mistaken beliefs about self leading to bad decisions which culminate in destructive action that take us back to mistaken beliefs and so on and so on.

As you're about to take on the challenge and adventure of fatherhood, or perhaps you have already made the plunge and are a new father, do yourself and your child a huge favor: examine or if you have already done that, re-examine the beliefs you hold about yourself.

"Am I good, smart, strong, healthy, honest, wise, loving, fair, self-assertive, generous, mindful, user-friendly to myself enough to be a father?

"What messages did I grow up with that could have stolen the sun from my sky as a child and adolescent? What crap did I start heaping upon myself because someone had no faith in me or that I hadn't lived up to his or her expectations?

"What are the worst attributes I have and what's my proof that they truly represent me? Am I more prone to swallow deprecating comments about me and hear only the negative comments, or am I also available habitually for the good news, the appreciations, and the acknowledgments?

"Do I have the self-confidence to take on the challenge of becoming a good-enough, empathic, caring father who may know little but is willing to learn from the appropriate sources and who can tell the difference between worthy and worthless sources?

"Am I usually optimistic, pessimistic, or realistic about my talents, expertise, shortcomings, and flaws?

"Do I tend to believe that people like me because I'm a good team player or because they want something from me?"

This list is open-ended. Find the questions that are most obviously and most frequently damaging to the way you think of yourself and of your self-worth. If you come up with a lot of negative answers as you're taking stock of your beliefs about yourself, you urgently need to revisit those beliefs and look for the evidence, tangible and concrete evidence, that supports those nasty beliefs. I predict that your negative beliefs rest on much less evidence than on garbage others heaped on you as you were growing up. Examine who may be currently in your life who keeps on contributing to this pile of shit.

Some of the negative beliefs you hold about yourself may come from matters completely out of anyone's control. They may have visited your youth and claimed squatter's right on your life: poverty, war, illness, death of a loved one, prejudice, discrimination, etc., in short, what insurance companies call "acts of God" (many of them are actually affronts to God, whatever is your faith). If you can't practice treating yourself with practical empathy, you may need the services of a professional or the support and wisdom of a men's group, or both.

Just remember well: if you want to be a hands-on, loving, and committed dad, you'll have to reinvent many of the beliefs you hold about yourself, so that on the strength of more realistic beliefs you'll be in line to make good-enough decisions about what you will and won't do. I wish more than anything that you learn to assess yourself realistically, if you are not yet in the habit of doing so. When all is said and done, and even before, I'm good enough, neither beast nor angel.

Slow down your reaction before you are inclined to act, asking: "Do I really want to do this? Will I think a year from today that this was a wise decision?" If not, then it isn't wise now either.

Ultimately, it all points to one fact: men have written themselves out of their own script as fathers, and only men can put themselves back in.

Be a leader in your own life.

Be a good-enough father to yourself so you can be one to your child. This means that, at times, you'll have to stand up for yourself, even to your partner. If you're like most men, you'll be apprehensive to do that for fear of losing her love. Let me tell you, if it is that easy to lose, you don't have it in the first place. If her love is conditional on you continuing to be an ATM or a doormat, your relationship needs serious spring cleaning. My guess is that she wants your love as much as you want hers.

I'd like to end this chapter by suggesting that your challenge is to learn to love yourself, your partner, and your children in a way that you all will value your contributions and presence more.

PART III

SNAPSHOTS

CHAPTER 49

TOXIC MESSAGES

Like many fathers, mine had a string of sayings that I loathed. Some cut to the quick, instantly and deeply. Others just made my heart sink. One way or another, they all said I was a disappointment, and that no matter what I did from this moment on I would never be good enough.

I'll give you my father's top ten sayings to make his kid feel crummy. To me, they're important, if for no other reason than to serve as reminders never to use them on my own kids. I'm quite sure some of these gems will be familiar to many of you. Or else, this recitation will trigger a memory of the top ten heartbreakers of your own childhood. Now that you are or are about to become a father, you will want to set up an armed sentry at your vocal chords, because these phantoms erupt totally unpredictably.

1. *If it was good enough for my father and my father's father and if it's good enough for me, it should be good enough for you.*

I'm not sure I ever believed him or trusted his insight on this one. His father allegedly was a strict autocrat, and my hunch is that my father was none too pleased with his dad's style of parenting. Still, he was passing down to his son the only thing he knew, the best way he knew how.

The logic of the saying is questionable. What was good enough for our ancestors should never be good enough for us. Times change, and it's not how the world works. Saying it to your child is nothing more than a destructive and annoying remark. And it only works to silence the kid if she's too young to respond.

2. *Do as I say, not as I do!*

This unique lesson in hypocrisy would certainly not be worth passing down, except for the fact that pronounced with the right intonation and at the appropriate time, it might not be all that bad. Charitably, the saying means that despite our best efforts we're unable to measure up to our own standards, and that we have every reason to believe that our child could be more successful. At its worst, it says, "I have no idea what I'm doing, not that it's any of your business, and I want you to follow my orders to the letter, blindly and unquestioningly."

For some reason, the room in my house reserved as my study is always in a state of chaos. Yet, for years I insisted that my kids keep their rooms neat and tidy. My son, who has always excelled in messiness, said one day: "Your study is as messy as my room." I was taken aback since I had not consciously realized it until that moment. I replied, rather meekly, "I work long hours and I don't have the time to tidy up." But what I almost said, was "Do as I say, not as I do." It is actually quite fascinating how phrases you have never used in your whole life stand ready to jump out at the right provocation, "right" being circumstances in your deepest memory that remind you of an incident in your youth.

3. *This hurts me more than it hurts you.*

You use this when you deny your child something he desires badly or, as in my case, when I was about to get the strap from my father. This is one of those statements that can only make sense to a parent. To articulate it to one's child is a waste of one's time, no more effective than breathing in and breathing out. I was no more than five years old when I first asked myself: "How does he know how much I hurt? And how come I am screaming in pain while he's quite cool about it all?" There is nothing in the memory bank for a child to draw on to make sense of such an inane assertion.

And yet it is often true that when we deny something to our child, it's we the parents who are left with the pain. While the child will be skipping off in a few minutes to a new adventure, the parent will be stuck in one spot, sucking on his guilt for days.

4. *When you grow up, you'll understand and thank me for it.*

This can be a prelude to a spanking, or denial of material or service, or prolonged incarceration. What the parent is saying is that you don't have enough sense to appreciate what's coming to you. What you view as punishment is really a reward.

Although in many cases the statement may be perfectly truthful, it is not in the child's lexicon to comprehend the depth and complexity of our intentions. Black and white may be similar in that black is the absence of white but such philosophical refinements are not of interest to a young child. So when we say something is white while the child perceives it as black, we're invalidating his feelings. Hence, the statement downgrades, and is painful. Hence it's cruel and should be eliminated.

Recently, a man and his adult daughter came to see me, seeking help in their reconciliation, having not spoken to each other for many years. The young woman, harboring years of resentment, confronted her father with a catalogue of cruel acts she had suffered at his hands from the time she was little. "I know," he said. "How else could I teach you a lesson? Now that you've become a mother, mark my words, one day you'll do the same for your daughter. Look how well you turned out." I told them it wouldn't be a quick fix.

5. *You're just a kid.*

This comment is sometimes said lovingly. When accompanied by a warm gaze and soft caressing, it will do no harm. But it can also be delivered in such a way that the kid feels not quite a member of the human race. In my mind, since I already knew what my father thought of me, being just a kid meant that I was not quite worthy of being his son. This minus sign in front of my name, reinforced by a thousand phrases like it, haunted me through most of my childhood and many of my adult years.

6. *Just who do you think you are?*

"Obviously the scum of the earth, judging by your tone." The presumption is that I am transgressing my rightful station in life, and that I need taking down a notch or two.

Should you be tempted to unleash this question on your child, ask yourself: "Who is this kid, really?" You'll quickly realize as your temper cools that this is the child you brought into this world, whom you love, and whom you want to endow with a healthy quantity of self-confidence.

7. *I'm doing this for your own good.*

Invariably, I knew that whatever came next, I would not be thankful for it, now or ever.

As parents, we all know that unpopular decisions need to be made from time to time. We also know that any child beyond the age of two is not going to take it lying down. Although you try to soften it with an explanation, your reasoning often is ignored because the child has too much invested in maintaining the status quo.

Rather than continuing the discussion, my approach has been some-thing like this: "Julie, you have to go to bed now. You haven't been able to wake up in the morning because you go to bed too late. Let's talk about it again tomorrow when you come home from school." Or, with your teenager: "Johnny, I explained why you can't borrow the car now that your license has been suspended. But if you want to talk about it, let's set time aside for just that. How about, say, Thursday after supper?" The common thread is postponing the discussion to a calmer place, giving time for reason to sink in. I would venture to say that in no more than one in twenty occasions does the promised discussion even take place.

Be honest with your kid and treat her with respect. Put your-self in her place. If you do, you won't insult her intelligence by asking her to agree with you in principle when you're doing some-thing hurtful to her. Even if perfectly justifiable, it is merely an at-tempt to dilute your responsibility by asking the child to concur in her punishment. It cannot be done. A bitter pill is a bitter pill.

8. *When I want your opinion, I'll ask for it.*

My father's variation on this theme: "When you speak to me, keep your mouth shut." There's no comeback to this insult for the younger child.

I have five children, four of whom can debate with the skill of union arbitrators. The fifth is still too young but catching up rap-idly. There's no shortage of unsolicited opinions and suggestions, flying left and right, all of which I like to try to respectfully con-sider, most of the time. In fact, our house is only quiet when the kids are asleep. I like that.

I have always suspected that people without power in their private worlds have kids in order to have at least one person they can boss around. At home, they wield a big stick. We must try not to be one of them. When we denigrate our child's opinion, we're catering to the lowest common denominator. The child needs to be free to voice an opinion without fear of being trampled on.

9. *You're a liar, and liars become thieves and thieves become killers and killers end up on the gallows.*

"Because I uttered an untruth I would suffer an ignoble death. Is he really worried about my future?" Of course I never queried him about what he really meant. We were never close enough for that. But I know my dad had a very dark view of his own station in life. During his whole life, he'd worked mostly as a sales clerk, just like his parents and grandparents had done. In his own assessment, none of them amounted to anything. Above all, he was afraid of authority or of anybody in uniform or who had some official status. He did not report to the communist authority every penny he made, with the result that he was constantly in fear of getting caught.

Accept it as hard fact that your kids will occasionally lie, to you and to everyone else, just to see what they can get away with. If it's more pernicious than that, we should examine whether we've made it safe for them to tell the truth. Also, if we express the slightest doubt on those occasions when they are telling the truth, they might as well lie since they conclude that there's no downside to lying.

In one of the courses I taught at the University of Toronto, I gave the students an assignment. They had to go twenty-four hours without telling a lie, however small, and to refrain from lies of omission. Over several years of teaching this course, there was not a single student who successfully completed the assignment. And when they fell off the wagon, it was with their closest friends and family members.

10. *One day, you'll be sorry . . . after I'm gone. You'll cry where nobody sees you.*

I do miss my father, even if now and then I criticize him. And, yes, I'm apt to cry for him when the mood strikes me, whether I'm seen or not.

I would be a much better son, now that I'm a father. I bet I could even learn from him a thing or two, never mind all the things I could teach him. I would love to teach him about relaxing around his son. Not every transgression is a nuclear event. I'd love to show him that in spite of his fears I turned out well, which means that he had done a good-enough job. I'd love to put my arm around his stooped shoulder and tell him: "Dad, the war is over. We won."

CHAPTER 50

FAST FOOD FOR THOUGHT

1. THE NOT-SO-MERRY-GO-ROUND

Conversation between two girls, about four to five years old, at a playground:

Girl A: Your daddy yells at you a lot. My daddy never yells at me. He says all the time, "I love my little girl, my little girl is a good little girl."
Girl B: I guess my daddy doesn't love me. He whacks me on the bum. He says I'm bad.
Girl A: My daddy doesn't whack me. He thinks I am good. Does it hurt?
Girl B: A lot. I'm bad. I am real bad.
Girl A: Your daddy doesn't love you?
Girl B: I guess not. When I grow up I'll become more bad. What will happen to me then?

This was one of the saddest conversations I ever heard. At the tender age of five, this little girl has come to the conclusion that she is bad and therefore not lovable, not even by her daddy. Pay heed to the words; they are all important. She is not saying that her father is angry with her for having done something bad. The child's way of making sense of her father's attitude and behavior is by concluding that there was something wrong with her.

It can get quite complicated. Simply, articulated in the child's voice: "My daddy thinks I'm bad, so he doesn't love me. Therefore I must be bad, so I feel bad." What she would need to tell her dad, if by some magic she had the maturity and wisdom: "I'm good and you don't love me; therefore, you're bad so I won't love you."

We must try to avoid communicating to our children, at any age, that our love is conditional on their doing one thing or another, or being one thing or another. Unconditional love is particularly hard for dads to pull off. In the reciprocating world most working dads live in and because they live by rules of fairness and retribution, they seem to have a hard time shedding the moral principles of the workplace when they enter the home. Moreover, they believe that they must teach the rules of engagement to their children in order to protect them from being crushed in the outside world. Yet, we must remember that conditional love is a huge burden for the child. She can never rest assured that no matter what, her daddy will always love her, which can shake her confidence to the core, leading to a career of anxiety and insecurity.

How many times have you heard a father (or a mother) say to a child: "I love you, sweetheart, you're a good girl"? While this sounds benign, it can send the message to the child that "I love you because you're good," and not "I love you because you are." Of course a lot depends on the tone and inflection. If you deemphasize "I love you" and emphasize "You're a good girl," you might as well be telling her "I love you because you're good, and only if you're good."

Make sure that however angry you are at your child, your love is never in question.

In the same vein, try to think clearly and consciously about the roots of your disappointment. Inevitably, your child will disappoint you on occasion. Even if you feel she hasn't tried hard enough, even if you think she is capable of a much better performance, your disappointment is yours and not the child's. You have put an expectation on her that she has not lived up to, or perhaps cannot live up to. So, love your child for who she is and not for who she should be. If she can't deliver, she becomes miserable. And so will you.

2. I WAS A PUSHER IN SOUTHERN CALIFORNIA

If you are a real dad, not just a biological father, you'll pay attention to your child as well as his friends. You may think that your kid would be jealous and begrudge the time and attention you devoted to his buddies. Far from it. I can just about guarantee that he will appreciate you the more, especially if you forgo comparing him negatively to them. Your attention to the entire menagerie will raise your child's stock on the playground and, later, in his team. My son remembers fondly the times I spent coaching his soccer team. The fact that our team won the league championship didn't hurt. I was the only parent who was out there on the field with his team every Wednesday evening and Sunday morning. The other parents? Maybe they were glad to have time for extra work, for making ends meet. Or maybe they were just sipping a cappuccino or watching TV.

The best illustration of what I'm saying took place much earlier, when my first daughter, Cybèle, was about three. Every Saturday I took her to a nearby park, just the two of us. Those were glorious days. I taught her how to ride our German shepherd, Pitic, something he too seemed to enjoy. We would go to the university campus, lie down on the top of a mound, and roll down the plush Southern California grass. Or I'd take her to Child's Estate in Santa Barbara around Christmas time and watch Santa come down in a helicopter.

But the greatest fun for her was in the middle of an everyday afternoon at the local playground, when all her little friends would congregate around the swing set. I did the pushing, which earned me the title of "the swing set pusher." I probably got more pleasure from pushing the swing than any of them riding it, partaking in their squeals of delight as they soared higher and higher. And the more her friends seemed to love it, the bigger grew the grin on my little girl's face.

The long and the short of it is: show your kid, at least every now and then, that her friends are not just a source of noise and mess around the house but also a thrill and a delight. You'll be on a high each time you're around these intoxicating little guys and gals for whom life is a party. And guess what! You're invited.

3. A WORD ABOUT SMALL CHANGE

About twenty years ago, I saw a wonderful French film *Small Change* about childhood. The director, the late François Truffaut, had been a terribly abused child, documented in another of his films, *400 Blows*. *Small Change* was a wishful fantasy about children growing up safely in a small town where everyone was mindful of a child's birthright to a healthy, compassionate and fun way of being raised. More than anything, the parents were empathic to the fragility and vulnerability of children, without as much as one abusive parent in town. The only instance of maltreatment happened out of town, to a boy who was regularly beaten by his demented mother. His lot made no sense to the other kids in his class—not one of them ever having heard a harsh word, let alone been smacked.

Even in this idyllic setting there were instances where Truffaut skillfully demonstrated what seemed on the surface significant lapses of empathy or compassion but turned out to the child's advantage after all. One of these instances has stuck firmly in my mind.

The chief of police and his wife were preparing to take their six-year-old girl, Sylvie, for a festive Sunday lunch at a restaurant, all dolled up in their Sunday best. Sylvie in preparation for the big event diligently cleans her elephant-shaped purse with a wet scrub brush. The result is a huge mess. When her father sees Sylvie all ready to go, he gently reminds her that she can't go to a nice restaurant with that filthy rag bag. Instead, he offers her one of his wife's own purses. But Sylvie holds out: she is going with her bag and no persuasion can move her. Finally, somewhat dismayed, the father pronounces the dreaded ultimatum with exemplary calm. "Sylvie, chèrie, you take one of mommy's bags or we're going to leave you at home." Sylvie retorts, with a huge smile on her face, "I don't mind." She knows either way she has won. She either gets to take her own purse or stays at home, without giving in, and she has special plans for staying behind. When her parents disappear past the building's front gate, she takes her father's bullhorn to the window facing an internal courtyard and makes the damning announcement, loud enough to wake the dead: "I'm hungry, I'm hungry, I'm hungry. My parents went to the restaurant and they locked me in without anything to eat." Within seconds, the outraged neighbors improvise a pulley system. When she pulls in the loaded basket, she muses, beaming: "Everyone was looking at me." And she has the best meal of her life together with a big moral victory.

My purpose in relating this story is to highlight the importance of letting the child win sometimes when there's no really dangerous consequence. If your young child, as young as three or four, asserts herself by wearing something that frazzles your sense of fashion, choose to take a small loss in exchange for a huge gain. The child needs to feel that her opinions and preferences matter. This of course is contrary to the adage that if you give an inch, she'll take a mile. But in fact most kids raised with clear, consistent, and empathetic rules are happy to take the occasional inch. They wouldn't even dream of the mile; they wouldn't know what to do with it. Your kid is wiser than you give her credit for. Extend that credit, and you'll find that she is a good risk.

4. FATHER'S MILK

We're learning increasingly in the literature about the different and unique influences moms and dads have on their children. In the right proportions, they're of equal value to the child. From father they learn more playfulness. And true enough, women through the ages have been referring to men somewhat condescendingly as never growing up, that boys will be boys. Well, undoubtedly, this is true of many men. But I believe what they're referring to is the taste men have for playfulness, for gadgets, for "getting down." Hence, you'll see many a father rolling on the carpet, mock wrestling with a young child. Others will climb the jungle gym with junior, hanging upside down like bats, without a moment's concern for potential harm. Are they irresponsible? Most often not. They are constitutionally more likely to take chances than moms, but if you look carefully the risks are minimal and necessary for the child's development. Occasionally, if their kid falls and scrapes a knee, the dad will check it out, clean it, hug the child, and encourage her to resume the fun. Under similar circumstances, the mom would be more likely to pamper, taking the child home for rest and recovery. Many mothers choose not to look when the father teaches junior skiing, bicycling, or roller-blading. From fathers, children learn courage, stick-to-it-ness, adventure, exerting their bodies, coordination, and competitiveness with a desire for competence. From moms, they typically learn sensitivity and manners, hygiene, the art of listening, and presenting their best qualities in social interactions. The child who has a good mix of parenting styles is a very lucky child indeed, and one destined for a balanced life.

On a personal note, I've told my children a thousand times over that I would support all their reasonable choices: that what I wished for them in all their endeavors is not to be best, but competent enough. I still believe that is the wisest stance for a parent to take. Lack of competence when I was a young child earned me humiliation, fear, shame, and at times exclusion and even beatings.

5. YOUR CHILD'S CANDID CAMERA

Robin Williams in his brilliant film *Mrs. Doubtfire* provides us with a piece of unimpeachable evidence that our kids watch us with hawk eyes when they see us interacting with their moms and that they listen with every fiber to pick up what we say about her to others.

Before anything else, I'd like to offer my rule of thumb on the subject: whenever you speak unkindly about Mom, your child will hurt. If you try to ally your child against her, he'll have no safe place to go because either way she turns, she'll have to betray one of you. So watch your tongue as if you're on *Candid Camera*.

In *Mrs. Doubtfire*, due to irreconcilable parenting values, Robin Williams and Sally Fields split up. Williams, in the best portrayal of the old cliché that love is not enough, wisdom and consistency being just as indispensable, gets weekly access to his children. His wife has a feverish abhorrence for his parenting philosophy. So fearful is she of his influence that she habitually shows up before the allotted time to pick up the kids. When one night Williams and the children are still having dinner, they hear the mother's car pull into the driveway. The children are about to get up to leave, but Williams orders them to sit down while blasting them in his frustration: "Sit down, I said! After all, you're my goddamn kids, too." When Mom walks in, Natty, the four-year-old, exclaims: "Yeah, Mom, we're his goddamn kids, too." It is a sad scene in a funny movie because everybody loses in this exchange. The kids see the parents denigrating each other.

So, according to another cliché, if you can't say anything nice, say nothing, and don't speak badly about their mom, even through insinuation. The kids are on to you and for sure will save it for a later day. If they accumulate enough of this, they will either conclude that Mom is a bad person and a bad mom, or they will choose to side with her, a lose-lose situation.

By all means, vent your feeling and your anger, but do it in private, to a confidante or in a psychotherapist's office. Don't let it fester. If you notice that you're accumulating a list of grievances, however small or trivial, there is a critical number beyond which the grievances not only grow in quantity but also become mountainous, overshadowing everything you think or do. Your bile will leak all over your child.

One dad was very angry with his wife for some anti-male attitude she had expressed. One day, while they were watching the news with their five-year-old (big mistake: five-year-olds have no business watching the news), the broadcaster reported a new development in the Clinton-Lewinsky melodrama. Here is how the conversation unfolded in my client's living room:

Mom: That Clinton is a no good son-of-a-bitch. No woman's safe with him.

Dad: And Lewinsky? I suppose she is a model of virtue, fucking her way to the top. Women are going overboard! They deserve a good old-style flogging if you ask me.

Son: (bursting into tears and hugging Mommy) Why do you want to hurt my mommy?

My client felt like a jackass afterwards. The child heard the word "flogging" and put it together with my client's threatening tone. Equally importantly, the battle of the sexes has found a new battleground—his home. There was work to be done!

Do whatever is necessary to shield your child from your resentment toward his mom.

6. "LOVE, HONOR, AND OBEY." (WHAT'S WRONG WITH THIS PICTURE?)

"It is our duty to bring up our children to love, honor and obey us. If they don't they must be punished, otherwise we would not be doing our duty." (R. D. Laing, *Knots*, p. 3)

What is odd in this formula is that it lumps together "love" and "obey." I don't see a direct link between the two. Obedience is the learned submission of one's personal freedom to another's will. We seldom if ever surrender it voluntarily. Children kick and scream and cave in only after they feel beaten or too scared to continue to assert themselves. The odds are not in their favor. Other, more fragile children, take a short cut to obedience without passing kicking and screaming. I have a fellow in my group, Keith, who went straight to obedience practically from the cradle because he was smart, intuitive, and observant and realized that there was really no money in asserting his right to free will. The cost? He became old before he had a chance to be young. By his father's assessment, Keith was born an old man. The truth is that he had no option; for surrendering one's youthful vigor and spunk is the end result of not staking claim to personal freedom.

What version of love extracts such a heavy toll from a child? Why would a caring father want to break the spirit of his child? Some see the world as a jungle. For them, it's to dominate or be dominated. I can't tell you how often I've heard mostly older fathers mouth the opinion that you must show your child who is boss or they take over. Children are power-hungry little beasts.

In reality I have never seen a child take more power than the parents were willing to afford them. At times, if they have too much power, it's not because they want, demand, or extort it. It happens when the parents think that giving free rein to their children is a caring and democratic way to raise them.

The naked truth is that children want less power rather than more. I will never forget the words of a forty-year-old woman who in the course of an interview about her dad said, "What I think was great with the way our father brought us up was that we always knew who he was, what were his values, and where were the limits. No, he didn't threaten, yell, or hit. Instead, in his usual, quiet way he explained to us what he didn't want us to do and what was the reason behind the limits he set. None of this 'Do what I say because I am your father.' Life was very clear, simple, and safe. Yeah, Father was an easy man to read, consequently an easy man to love."

In short, if you resolve not to fear your child's fantasized urge to take over the roost, you won't have to demand obedience. And if you can forgo domination, love will flow naturally, and he or she will honor your wisdom and your person. Then you will have done your duty as a father. Knowing the bulk of the late Scottish psychiatrist R. D. Laing's work and his fathering philosophy, I believe that his quote is not to be taken literally. To the contrary, there is a strong likelihood that he meant the opposite: we do our duty as fathers when we don't demand obedience from our children and inspire love and honor by behaving lovingly and honorably.

It is the father's job to teach his child to respect him by setting a good example. If he doesn't do that, he doesn't deserve his child's respect. If you want your child to eat nutritious food instead of junk, set the example and don't eat a cheeseburger with fries and a Coke and expect the kid to dine on tofu, carrots, and wheat juice. If you want to teach him the value of a tidy room, make sure that yours doesn't look like the inside of a dumpster and claim that you work all day and have no time to keep your room straight, whereas the lazy good-for-nothing lad does just that, nothing. If you want to teach the child the importance of honesty, refrain from bragging to your friends in front of junior about how you beat the taxman out of a big one.

If, on the other hand, you try to spare him the hardship of fig-uring out the maze of your value system and opt for being loosey-goosey, he still won't respect you because he won't find your backbone even with a search light. What your kid will want from you is honesty, clarity, reasonable boundaries, consequences for his devious or destructive violations, firm and empathic leadership. You do that for a few decades and he'll respect you. As for honor, I don't really know the value of it in a father-son relationship. Love and respect will do the trick, thank you very much.

7. FACING THE FEAR OF FATHERHOOD

I've never met a young man who was fearless at the prospect of becoming a father the first time around. With repetition this gets easier. First time, you come to the situation equipped mostly with fantasies and other people's stories. No more carefree, spontane-ous existence, getting up and having the whim of flying to New York for the weekend. Or being able to say "yes" to a friend's poker game without a second thought. Or to buying a new MP3 record-ing gadget for $500 without blinking an eye. Then, there's still the main event.

The main event is the arrival of a helpless new being in your life, who will be your responsibility. This new life will want, need, and deserve everything from you and your partner. Now, here's a scary prospect.

In earlier chapters, I've already addressed this topic in depth. Here, I want to share another memory with you that I found sooth-ing. It helped me get used to the presence of my baby before she even graced our home.

About three weeks before Cybèle was born, we installed all the baby furniture and decorations in what was to become the nurs-ery. We made it really pretty, in gender-neutral pale yellow and red and a burst of happy colors. This was in 1966, in hippy Berkeley. When the work was done, my wife went to sleep exhausted. But I stayed in the room, sitting on the floor, trying to imagine our baby in the crib. And soon enough, I could almost hear the cooing of an infant. Pretty soon, I began to sing, "Hush little baby, don't you cry."

Then I fell asleep on the thick yellow carpet. When I woke up, my first awareness was disappointment at not seeing a baby in the crib. The second was relief—I was definitely not ready for her yet.

But I did feel much less anxious. In the following weeks, I made a point of spending time everyday in the nursery. As days went by, I grew increasingly peaceful about the pending arrival of my baby. In fact, about ten days before her birth, I detected a buzz of impatience in my whole body. I wanted her to fill the nursery, the house, and my life with her presence. I got into the habit of talking to her in the nursery about my dreams, plans, ambitions, and whatever else came into my mind.

That's all for now. I've got to run to my baby. She's now thirty-five, and expecting. Oh, the joys of fatherhood, they never stop giving. Fear of becoming a father? What fear?

8. THE SPORT NAZI

Recently, I overheard a conversation between two men waiting to board a flight in Vancouver. One of them, a man in his mid-thirties, was saying to his traveling companion, "The only thing I really worry about raising my son is getting into bad shit: drugs, crime, and booze. He's only seven now but hardly a day goes by without something reminding me that I, as a father, can do only so much. The rest is out of my control."

"I have two kids, a boy, twenty-two, and a girl, nineteen," answered the other, a strapping fifty-something fellow. "I had my days of white-knuckled parenting but ultimately it was pretty smooth riding. From the time they could walk I got them involved in organized sports. I've been a hockey nut all my life, so hockey it was. My kids learned to skate practically as they began to walk. Then we added swimming, baseball, and karate. Some friends, mostly women, called me a Sport Nazi. But I paid no attention. I knew that if the kids learned to spend their energy in sports there would be little time to waste on hanging out and getting into trouble."

"And they did it voluntarily?" the younger one asked incredulously. "My little guy drags his feet every time I take him swimming."

"I never just took them swimming or anything else," said the other man. "I did it with them. I got up with them at 5 a.m. and stayed on the ice as hockey coach. You've got to put your ass on the line or you'll have no credibility. And that's another thing. In organized sports there is always a coach."

Healthy minds, healthy bodies—an ancient recipe that still works.

9. THE BOOK IS THE ANSWER

Some twenty years ago, I attended a passionate lecture by Nobel Peace Prize laureate Elie Wiesel. He was hosted by a Jewish organization committed to perpetuate Judaism and its values. The man who introduced Wiesel expressed very strong concern about the number of Jews lost through intermarriage and secularism. Then Wiesel said, "I've no fear for the Jewish people's future, provided we instill proper values in our children. We're the people of the Book. Therein lies the answer. Take your children to Sunday school for Jewish education. And then stay with them. Don't run off for a cappuccino or to the gym while your child is being read stories. Be there with them so he and you can share the joy of learning. Then go home and talk about what you both have learned."

Take your child to the bookstore or to the library. Pick out some books you both enjoy reading or just paging through. As you explore their content, you also help your child develop a world of imagination.

Sacha and I don't miss an opportunity to make a dash for the bookstore. It may be a Borders-type megastore where one can pick a bunch of books, lie down on the floor, spread out and go at it for hours. Or just as enjoyable is a musty second-hand bookstore, with its helter-skelter chaos, where you two can revel in the pleasure of discovering a hidden treasure.

As your child grows, she'll learn new words from books, along with proper sentence structure, which will give her the confidence needed for self-expression. And a child who's comfortable with speaking up learns to feel good about herself in any setting or situation.

When you read to your young child, she will be riveted by your voice and the images you show her. The memory of this ritual she will cherish for the rest of her life. A unique intimacy will grow between the two of you. And as a bonus, you'll find it soothing and restoring at the end of a busy day.

10. A MIND IS A TERRIBLE THING TO WASTE

"At four, Erin began to talk back," explained Will. "It seemed to me that even at that tender age she wanted to take over. And she was stubborn as hell. Well, we just couldn't let that happen. It wouldn't have worked. All my life I had bosses, and everybody has a boss, so I had to teach her that right then I was her boss."

"I agree, Will," I said to this man of fifty-two who was in my office to "help" his adult daughter make peace with what she considered an abused childhood. "Every young child needs to know that a safe parent is in charge. By safe I mean one who is on her side, one that will protect her from harm. But when the protector gets into the habit of hitting her, she no longer sees him as either safe or on her side. These are conflicting messages she's receiving. What do you think?"

"If you twist the situation to mean that I was a crazy-making father, sure it sounds pretty bad," replied Will. He was a former police officer in a small town in Southwestern Ontario, not used to being argued with. "But I've a different perspective on it. If she learned that minding her Ps and Qs would keep her out of trouble, she'd never get smacked. And it was my responsibility to make sure that she was clear on the rules. Besides, Erin was way ahead of herself. By the time she was eight, she argued about everything. We couldn't just let her go wild. What would that lead to? She insisted on having her own mind about everything."

"Perhaps you had on your hands an independent thinker, the kind that can become a great leader. But you told me last time that you used to get brutal beatings from your father, pretty much as a steady diet. Did that make you end up with less of your mind?"

"Hell, no." He sounded feisty and a more than a shade proud of himself. "When I was old enough, around nine, I began to retaliate. When he'd beat me, I'd steal his money, piss in his beer, and bend his golf gear. I just had to be smarter."

"Precisely. A young mind is a terrible thing to waste. You can't snuff it out. You can only twist it."

Will grew silent. He was lost in thought for a few minutes. "Gotcha, doc." He sounded genuine. "So I twisted my little girl's mind. I'm responsible and guilty as charged. What do I do now?"

"What you are doing. Take responsibility, express regret, and ask her what she needs and wants from you. Then give it to her in good heart, without defensiveness."

Make sure you won't have to have a conversation like this with your child's therapist. Rejoice in the vitality of your child's mind and do whatever you can to nurture it.

EPILOGUE

Now that you've read this book, you know a little bit about being a mindful father. Everything you've learned about yourself, your partner, and the relationship between the three of you is but a drop in the ocean. What I hope goes beyond that is the awakened curiosity inside the core of you that will provoke your thirst for conscious awareness for the rest of your life.

Being a father is but one facet of a man's life. But it may be the most vital and influential since his actions cross generations and will reverberate through history even if no books are written about him and even if he sees himself as just a drone in the colony of man. For your child you are the king of kings, the most important man in the history of the world.

And yet we must maintain a sense of humor about our exalted position. We've done nothing to earn it, nor can any human being live up to it. At some point, a child must reconcile her image of her father with his imperfect humanity. Where these contrary viewpoints meet, we shall find wails and the gnashing of teeth. These go with the territory and their origins are not of our making.

So, now that you have survived your first experience, what about having another child?

It may not come as a surprise that the next experience will not be a duplication of the first. That would be too easy. Here are some of the reasons:

1. You're not the same man. You have lived more days, and you have learned plenty from your first experience.

2. Your second kid will not be a clone of the first. Don't be surprised if he turns out the exact opposite.

3. Your partner has changed, and predictably she will be unpredictable in different ways.

4. There will be more than one child in the family with the complexity of added dynamics and cross linkages.

5. Having succeeded once, you'll be more relaxed and more able to enjoy being a dad.

Without a doubt, the parenting years have been the best hundred years of my life so far. A childless couple is not a family in my humble opinion. Which does not mean that every couple should have a child. My point is: don't dismiss the thought because of ridiculous arguments prompted by fear of parenting.

Some men say they are too selfish to have children, meaning that they're too preoccupied with themselves or their careers to devote the time. Others maintain that the world is an imperfect place and it's overpopulated to boot.

Poppycock. *Not* to have children is the real sacrifice. The world may be an imperfect place but one that is immeasurably improved by the presence of children. And it's hardly overpopulated. We just have too many gadgets.

Think about this. If all those who think that the world is too rotten a place for children abstained from having them, only those who made it into such a mess would procreate. Ain't that a scary thought?

Post Scriptum:
Where Have All
the Young Dads Gone?

Justine, a seven-year-old girl in the East Village of New York City, kissed her dad goodbye with the taken-for-granted knowledge that Daddy goes to work in the morning and comes home at night. And then they have fun till both Mommy and Daddy tuck her in with a story. This day, however, Daddy will not come home. Nor ever again.

Aman, a seven-year-old boy on a hillside in Afghanistan, went on with his life as he has done every day since he started school. He wished his father a good day and good health and off he walked towards the nearby village where the ramshackle hut called school was located. He fully expected the day to be like any other day— learning, playing, talking, having lunch, going home, and then going to sleep after having received his father's blessing for the night. This day, however, a great calamity happened overseas. A lot of people were dead and somebody who is supposed to be living in his country is accused of having caused their death. Now, most of the world is angry with his people. Nothing will ever be the same in his impoverished existence.

Mahmoud is a nine-year-old boy on a playground in San Francisco, California. He went to school as usual with his two best friends. And as usual, they were lost in heated discussion about the Giants' game, or a TV show from the night before, or in planning the soccer game that afternoon against their arch-rivals whom they just haven't been able to beat the last few outings. Then it happened. The principal's voice on the PA system was as pale as the piece of chalk in Mr. D'Onofrio's hand in his fourth grade class. The disembodied voice appeared to come from nowhere just like the plane that smashed into the flank of the World Trade Center. The rest of the day felt like a sudden grave illness. The schoolyard was nearly silent. Everyone was whispering as mourners do at a gravesite. The boy was wondering whether he should run home. But there would be no one there. His parents were at work. Should he call them at work? What could they do? What if he told them he was scared that people would blame him—and them—for this horrible crime. His body sensed grave danger in all its young fibers. He was old enough to know that his grandparents had come from Lebanon many decades ago and that Muslim terrorists were being blamed. He knew that people were going to be very angry with Arab-Americans. What about his two best friends, Guido and Jonathan? Will they also think that all Arabs are killers?

For the first time, the boy was not so happy to be who he was. Are they right, those who hate Arabs? Are they really bad, dangerous, and prone to violence? Is Allah behind the terrorists? Or were the terrorists deluded into thinking they were killing on His behalf? With the visceral intuitiveness of a child that can't be uttered in words, Mahmoud knew that nothing would ever be the same again.

Sacha, an eleven-year-old girl in Toronto, got up this day as every other day. Then she dressed and groomed herself and had breakfast of her mom's homemade strawberry smoothie, milk and cereal, and orange juice. She took her dog for a run around the block. Then she went off to school with her mom, expecting to have a great day with her new friends and new teacher in her new school. Daddy, as always, would pick her up at 3:20. They would do some errands, go for a treat, or for a browse-and-buy at the bookstore, then go home. Things went quite as anticipated. Except, at ten o'clock, the vice-principal came to the class and told the kids that a terrible attack was perpetrated on the World Trade Center in New York City and the Pentagon in Washington, D.C., and a lot of people were killed. When Daddy came to pick her up, he looked sad, worried, and very quiet. That night, they all watched a lot of TV together. Horrible images of destruction. "Daddy, is this going to be World War III? Are they going to bomb the building where you and Mom work? Are we going to be extinct?" Daddy said an emphatic "no" to each question, yet he and Mommy continued to sound and look very troubled. Sleep didn't come to her that night. She ended up seeking shelter in her parents' bedroom on an improvised bed on the floor. For her, too, nothing will be the same ever again.

Bandi, an eight-year-old boy, was walking down the middle of a street of his native Budapest with a bunch of other children and older folk. The militiamen on each side, some only teenagers, poked with their bayonets those who couldn't keep up. Now and then he had to step over the inert body of an old man or woman whose heart rebelled sufficiently against the harsh treatment to shut down. The sidewalks were lined with local residents whirling insult and scorn at the marchers. "They deserve what's waiting for them, they're vermin, bloodsuckers, goddamned greedy pigs . . . Jews. Shoot the bunch and dump them into the Danube." Bandi had heard these hateful words before and, as before, they made no sense to him. All the Jews he knew were poor, hard-working people, not hurting or bothering anyone. Yet, he learned that to be Jewish in 1944 in Budapest was dangerous. Everybody seemed to want the Jews dead, children and all. Perhaps they were guilty of something; perhaps they did deserve their fate, Bandi thought. Mom and Dad had already been deported and those still around seemed to be too scared to be bothered with his questions. He felt the chill of panic and shame, the chill of the damp darkness, for the rest of his life.

I know these children. Since March 19, 1944, I have been these children. We have been corralled into a pathetic cluster, defying time and geography. We have been the frontline victims of every act of war and terrorism. Our crime? We were children, the seeds of the future, which made us dangerous. But not to worry. We are not children anymore. We've become old before we had a chance to be young.

In one kind of war or another, waged by men, the children are left to wander in their young world like rudderless ships in the sea. Some of the sad young men are swept up by their cursed destiny, meted out by evil men, or the results of the actions of evil men. Others became the "lucky ones." They at least had a chance to put together their shattered lives, though never the same as before. Still others perish outright.

We all die some day; it is the price of being born. But we have an easier time integrating this bargain with life if we can take for granted that between our first and the last breath there will be countless moments of happiness and joy. For most young victims the odds of this happening are reduced. Which poses a particular challenge to fathering, for their entire lifespan.

Those who had been robbed of their chance to partake in giving and nurturing a new life have also been robbed of this ground level joy. This is a scandal. To cripple the spirit and mind of a young man with fear and trembling for his child's survival is an assault on the spirit. And yet, those who were afforded the opportunity to grapple with this anguish and chaos were the lucky ones.

In the tragedy of the World Trade Center, as in any war, misguided older men will order young men and even boys to put their lives on the line. Human history is built on the ashes of young boys and men who give their lives before they give new life, boys not deemed old enough to marry without parental permission, or drink a beer, or drive a car.

How is it that we haven't yet learned that there is something fundamentally unjust about ordering a boy to surrender his life for an ideal, a country, or a religion?

How is it that fathers who have enjoyed a long life have not grown sufficient compassion for their sons to protect them from getting killed or killing somebody else's child?

How is it that mothers don't throw their bodies across their front doors to block the path to those who greedily aim to rob their sons of their present and their future?

Young or future fathers who have read this book, I appeal to you in the name of all children, yours and mine, not to pick up arms, for it is inevitably going to cost children their lives, ours and theirs. Nothing is worth the death of one child. He who saves the life of one child saves a whole world.

I have witnessed, in one moment in history, in New York and Washington, D.C., the shredding of bodies, the shattering of hearts. To the thousand who perished, I wish to say that your spirit will survive forever. Your children and mine will make sure of that.

INDEX